AF408359

Introduction: Get Ready to See the Big Picture

Welcome to a year of big ideas. You probably have many questions about God. Is He real? Why did He make the stars? Why do bad things happen? These are not small questions. They deserve real answers.

This book uses something called Systematic Theology. That is a giant name for a simple idea. It means we take all the truths in the Bible and put them in order. Think of it like sorting a massive pile of building blocks. Once you group the pieces by color and shape, you can finally build something great. We are going to build a solid foundation for your faith.

Over the next 52 weeks, we will look at one big truth at a time. We will not just read a verse and move on. Instead, we will see how these truths fit into history and science. You will see how the Creator's plan touches every part of your daily life.

<u>Copyright 2026 - All rights reserved.</u>

The content contained within this book may not be reproduced, duplicated, or transmitted without direct written permission from the author or the publisher.

Under no circumstances will any blame or legal responsibility be held against the publisher, or author, for any damages, reparation, or monetary loss due to the information contained within this book, either directly or indirectly.

<u>Legal Notice:</u>

This book is copyright protected. It is only for personal use. You cannot amend, distribute, sell, use, quote, or paraphrase any part, or the content within this book, without the consent of the author or publisher.

<u>Disclaimer Notice:</u>

Please note the information contained within this document is for educational and entertainment purposes only. All effort has been executed to present accurate, up-to-date, reliable, and complete information. No warranties of any kind are declared or implied. Readers acknowledge that the author is not engaging in the rendering of legal, financial, medical, or professional advice. The content within this book has been derived from various sources. Please consult a licensed professional before attempting any techniques outlined in this book.

By reading this document, the reader agrees that under no circumstances is the author responsible for any losses, direct or indirect, that are incurred as a result of the use of the information contained within this document, including, but not limited to, errors, omissions, or inaccuracies.

Table of Contents

We will not talk down to you. You are old enough to hear the truth as it is. You will read stories that make sense and find ways to live out your faith every day. There are no boring lectures here. You will find the facts about the King of the universe.

Each week follows a simple pattern:

- **A Big Idea:** A clear truth to think about.

- **A Unique Verse:** A specific word from God to guide you.

- **A Real Story:** A look at how this truth works in the real world.

- **An Action Step:** Something you can do right now to grow.

By the end of this year, you will see the world in a new way. You will know why you believe what you believe. You will have the tools to talk about your faith with anyone. Let's get to work.

Part 1:
How We Know What Is True
(Bibliology)

"The Big Idea"

The Bible is a direct message from the Creator to you.

SCRIPTURE FOCUS

"All Scripture is God-breathed and is useful for teaching, rebuking, correcting and training in righteousness," - 2 Timothy 3:16

The Message in the Locker

Imagine you walk up to your locker at school. You see a small, folded piece of paper tucked into the door. You open it and realize it is a letter from the head coach of the best team in the country. He wrote your name at the top. He tells you exactly how to improve your game. He even shares a secret play that no one else knows.

You wouldn't just toss that paper in the trash. You would read it until you memorized every word. You would show your friends. Most importantly, you would do exactly what the letter said. Why? Because you know who sent it. The value of the message comes from the person who wrote it.

The Bible is that letter, but it is from someone much bigger than a coach. It is from the King of the universe. Some people think the Bible is just a collection of old stories or good advice. In Systematic Theology, we learn the truth. This book is "breathed out" by God.

What Does "Breathed Out" Mean?

When you speak, you use your breath to make sounds. If you hold your hand in front of your mouth while you talk, you can feel the warm air. This is what the Bible means when it says God "breathed" the scriptures.

God did not sit at a desk and pick up a pen. Instead, He used about 40 different men over a span of 1,500 years. Some were kings. Others were fishermen or doctors. God allowed them to use their own writing styles and their own languages. However, His Spirit guided their minds so perfectly that they wrote exactly what He wanted. Every fact is right. Every promise is true.

This is why we call the Bible the "Word of God." It is not a book about God. It is God speaking to us.

Why This Matters Today

Have you ever felt like you didn't know which way to go? Maybe you had a fight with a friend. Maybe you felt afraid of the future. In those moments, you don't need a guess or a "maybe." You need a solid answer.

Because God breathed out the Bible, it has authority. That means it is the final word on what is true. If God says you are loved, you are loved. If He says He will never leave you, He won't. You can trust the Bible more than the news, more than social media, and even more than your own feelings. Feelings change, but God's breath stays steady.

Talk It Over

1. If God wrote a book specifically for you, would you read it every day? Why or why not?

2. Why is it cool that God used regular people like fishermen to write His Word?

3. How does knowing the Bible is "God-breathed" change the way you listen to it at church?

Take Action

This week, find a quiet spot. Open your Bible to the book of Psalms. Read five verses out loud. As you read, remember that those words are God's breath. Ask Him to help you hear His voice as you read.

"The Big Idea"

The Bible is the only foundation that never moves or breaks.

SCRIPTURE FOCUS

"Your word is a lamp for my feet, a light on my path." - Psalm 119:105

The Midnight Hike

Have you ever tried to walk through a thick forest in the middle of the night? Without a moon or a flashlight, you cannot see anything. Every stick that snaps sounds like a giant monster. You might trip over a tree root or wander right into a cold stream. You feel lost because you have no way to see what is real and what is just a shadow.

The world can feel like that forest. People have many different ideas about how to live. One person might tell you that being famous is the most important thing. Another might say that you should only care about yourself. These ideas change all the time, just like the shadows in a dark forest. If you follow them, you will eventually trip.

God knew we would need help. He did not leave us to guess our way through life. He gave us a light. In Systematic Theology, we call this the "Sufficiency of Scripture." That is a big way of saying the Bible gives us exactly what we need to know the truth.

What Is a "Solid" Truth?

Think about math. Two plus two always equals four. It does not matter if you are happy, sad, or tired. It does not matter if you are in America or on the moon. It is a solid truth. It never changes.

The Bible is full of these solid truths. It tells us that God created the world. It tells us that every human being has value. It tells us that lying hurts people and that kindness builds them up. These are not just "opinions." They are the laws of how the world actually works.

Many people try to build their lives on things that shift. They build on their feelings, or on what is popular on the internet. But feelings change like the weather. One day you feel like a hero, and the next day you feel like a failure. If your truth changes every day, you will never feel safe. When you build your life on the Bible, you are standing on a rock. Even when the storms of life hit, a rock does not wash away.

Why Your Feet Need a Lamp

Look closely at the verse for this week. It says the Word is a lamp to your **feet**. It does not say it is a massive stadium light that shows you the next twenty years of your life.

A lamp for your feet shows you the very next step. It helps you make the right choice right now. Should you tell the truth about who broke the window? Should you stand up for the kid being teased at lunch? The Bible gives you the light to see those steps clearly. It points out the traps and shows you the safe path.

Talk It Over

1. What is one thing you used to believe when you were little that you know is not true now? (Like the tooth fairy!)

2. Why is it scary to trust your feelings when you are angry or upset?

3. How does the Bible act like a flashlight when you have to make a hard choice at school?

Take Action

Find a piece of cardboard or a heavy rock. Write the word **TRUTH** on it with a marker. Put it on your desk or by your bed. Every time you see it this week, remember that God's Word is your solid ground. It stays still even when everything else is moving.

"The Big Idea"

God has protected His Word so the message never changes.

"SCRIPTURE FOCUS"

"The grass withers and the flowers fall, but the word of our God endures forever." - Isaiah 40:8

The Cave of Wonders

In 1947, a young shepherd boy was looking for a lost goat in the desert. He saw a small opening in a cliff side. He threw a rock into the hole and heard a strange sound—clink! He didn't find his goat. Instead, he found old clay jars filled with ancient leather scrolls.

These are now called the Dead Sea Scrolls. They had been hidden in that dry cave for over 2,000 years. When experts studied them, they were shocked. They compared these ancient scrolls to the Bibles we use today. Even though thousands of years had passed, the words were almost exactly the same.

Some people think the Bible is like a long game of "telephone." You know how that goes. One person whispers, "The cat is on the mat," and by the time it reaches the last person, it sounds like, "The bat has a hat." But the Bible is not a game of telephone. The discovery in those caves proved that the Bible we read today is the same one people read in the time of Jesus.

How Did It Stay the Same?

Before printing presses and computers existed, people had to copy the Bible by hand. This sounds like a recipe for mistakes, right? But the people who copied the Bible, called scribes, were incredibly careful.

They didn't just write quickly. They counted every single letter on a page. If they were copying a page and realized they missed one letter, they would throw the whole page away and start over. They even knew which letter was the exact middle of the entire book. If the middle letter of their copy didn't match the middle letter of the original, they knew they had a problem.

But there is a bigger reason the Bible hasn't changed. God promised to protect it. Since the Bible is His message to us, He made sure that no king, no fire, and no mistake could ever delete it. Many people throughout history tried to destroy every Bible in the world. They failed every time.

Why This Matters for Your Faith

If the Bible changed every few hundred years, we could never be sure what God actually said. We would wonder if the promises were still true. But because God's Word "stands forever," we can be 100% sure.

When you read that God loves you, you don't have to wonder if that was a "copying error." When you read that Jesus rose from the dead, you can know that is a historical fact. The Bible is the most well-preserved book in the history of the world. No other ancient book has as many copies or as much evidence to back it up.

Talk It Over

1. Why do you think people tried to destroy the Bible in the past?

2. If you were a scribe, would you find it hard to start a whole page over just because of one tiny mistake?

3. How does knowing about the Dead Sea Scrolls help you trust the Bible more than a regular storybook?

Take Action

Find a very old book in your house or at a library. Look at the edges of the pages. Are they yellow? Are the covers worn? Books get old and fall apart, but the message inside the Bible stays brand new. This week, thank God that He kept His Word safe so you could read it today.

"The Big Idea"

God's Word is a perfect guide that never leads you the wrong way.

SCRIPTURE FOCUS

"Every word of God is flawless; he is a shield to those who take refuge in him." - Proverbs 30:5

The Maze and the Map

Imagine you are standing at the entrance of a giant corn maze. The walls are twice as tall as you. You can't see over them, and you have no idea which way to turn. If you just start running, you will probably end up at a dead end. You might get frustrated and feel like you are walking in circles.

Then, someone hands you a map. This is not just any map. It was drawn by the person who designed the maze. They know exactly where every path leads. They know where the traps are and where the exit is. If you follow that map, you will get through the maze every single time.

Life can feel like a giant maze. Every day you have to make choices. Should you join that group of friends? How should you react when someone is mean to you? What should you do with your time? The Bible is the map designed by the One who created life itself. Because He made you, He knows the best way for you to live.

Why "Every Word" Matters

Think about a GPS on a phone. It works because it has tiny, accurate details about every street and every turn. If the GPS was wrong about just one street corner, you could end up in a different city. You wouldn't trust a map that was "mostly" right. You need a map that is 100% right.

The Bible is 100% right. In Systematic Theology, we call this **Inerrancy**. That is a fancy word which means "without error." Because God is perfect, His Word is perfect. He does not include "maybe" or "I think so" in the Bible. He gives us the facts.

If we couldn't trust the Bible when it talks about history or science, we wouldn't be able to trust it when it talks about how to get to heaven. But because "every word" proves true, we can lean on the whole book. Whether the Bible is talking about the beginning of the world or how to treat your brother, you can be sure it is telling the truth.

A Shield for the Path

The second part of the verse in Proverbs says that God is a "shield to those who take refuge in him." When you follow the "map" of the Bible, it actually protects you. It keeps you from making choices that would hurt you or other people.

For example, the Bible says that "a soft answer turns away wrath." That is like a map telling you to take a left turn to avoid a fight. When you use kind words instead of yelling back, you are following the map. You are staying on the safe path. God's rules are not there to stop your fun. They are there to keep you safe and help you find real joy.

Talk It Over

1. Have you ever tried to build something without looking at the instructions? What happened?

2. If the Bible was only "mostly" true, how would that change the way you read it?

3. What is one "rule" in the Bible that you think actually helps keep people safe?

Take Action

Find a set of instructions for a board game or a toy. Look at how specific the steps are. This week, pick one specific instruction from the Bible—like "be kind to one another"—and follow it like a step on a map. See how it changes your day.

Nature shows us God's power, but the Bible tells us His heart.

"The heavens declare the glory of God; the skies proclaim the work of his hands." - Psalm 19:1

The Mystery of the Masterpiece

Imagine you are walking through an art gallery. You stop in front of a massive painting of a mountain range. The colors are so real you can almost feel the cold wind on the peaks. You notice tiny, perfect details—the way the light hits the snow and the shadow of a hawk circling a cliff.

You don't need to see the artist to know they exist. The painting itself is proof. You can tell the artist is skillful, patient, and loves beauty. You might even guess that the artist has traveled to high places. But you don't know the artist's name. You don't know where they live or why they painted this specific mountain. To find those things out, you would need to read the artist's biography or talk to them.

The universe is God's masterpiece. In Systematic Theology, we call this **General Revelation**. This means God has shown His power to everyone on earth through the things He made.

Science and the Signature

Some people think that science and the Bible are enemies. They think you have to choose one or the other. But that isn't true at all! Science is simply the study of how God's world works. When a scientist looks through a telescope at a galaxy millions of miles away, they are seeing God's "handywork." When a biologist looks through a microscope at the DNA inside a tiny cell, they are reading God's "code."

Everything in nature has a design. Think about the way a bird's wing is shaped for flight or the way the earth stays at just the right distance from the sun so we don't freeze or burn up. This isn't luck. It is the work of a brilliant Creator. Nature tells us that God is incredibly smart and more powerful than we can imagine.

The Missing Piece

Nature is like a giant "Hello!" from God. It lets us know He is there. But nature has limits. A beautiful sunset can tell you that God is creative, but it can't tell you that He wants to forgive your sins. A massive thunderstorm can tell you that God is powerful, but it can't tell you that He sent His Son, Jesus, to save you.

That is why we need the Bible. We call the Bible **Special Revelation**. While nature shows us God's work, the Bible tells us God's name. It tells us the "why" behind the "what." Nature is the beautiful cover of the book, but the Bible is the story inside. When we look at both, we see the full picture.

Talk It Over

1. If you could visit any place in nature (like the ocean, the desert, or the mountains), where would you go to see God's power?

2. What is one thing you can learn about God from a star that you can't learn from a textbook?

3. Why do you think God made the world so beautiful instead of just making it plain and gray?

Take Action

Go on a "Signature Hunt." Go outside or look out a window. Find three things that show God's design, it could be a leaf, a cloud, or even your own hand. Then, open your Bible and read a verse about God's love. Thank Him for showing Himself to you in both ways.

Part 2:
Who Is God?
(Theology Proper)

In this section, we are going to study the most important person in the universe. In theology, this is called Theology Proper. It is the study of God the Father: His character, His power, and what makes Him different from any other being.

There is only one true God, and He is in charge of everything.

"Hear, O Israel: The Lord our God, the Lord is one."

—Deuteronomy 6:4

The Throne Room

Imagine you go to a stadium to watch a championship game. On the field, there are players, coaches, referees, and thousands of fans in the seats. But there is only one person who owns the team and the stadium. There is only one person who has the final say on how things are run.

In the ancient world, people were very confused about who was in charge of the universe. They thought there was a god for the sun, a god for the rain, and a god for the trees. They lived in fear, trying to please many different "bosses."

But the Bible tells us a much better story. It tells us that there is only one God. He doesn't have to share His power with anyone. He doesn't have to check with a committee before He acts. He is the Only King. In Systematic Theology, we call this **Monotheism**. It means we believe in one God who created everything and rules over everything.

Why "One" Is a Big Deal

Think about your own family. If you had ten different parents all giving you different rules at the same time, you would be very stressed out! One parent says "go play," another says "do your homework," and another says "clean the kitchen." You wouldn't know who to listen to.

Because there is only one God, we can have peace. We don't have to wonder if the "god of the mountains" is mad at the "god of the valleys." We only have to listen to one Voice. Everything in the universe, from the spinning planets to the tiny ants in your backyard, answers to Him.

This one God is also a person. He isn't just a "force" or a "vibe." He has thoughts, feelings, and a plan. He is the King, but He is not a distant king who sits in a cold castle. He is a King who knows your name.

The King's Character

Since there is only one God, we should give Him our best. The verse in Deuteronomy says "The Lord is one" right before it tells us to love Him with all our heart, soul, and might.

If there were many gods, our love would be split up into little pieces. But because He is the only one, we can give Him all our loyalty. He is the original. Everything else, like money, sports, or even our favorite hobbies, can be good, but they are not God. They didn't make the world, and they can't save us. Only the King can do that.

Talk It Over

1. If you were a king or queen of a country, what is the first good rule you would make?

2. Why is it better to have one God who is in charge of everything instead of many gods who argue?

3. What are some things people today "worship" or treat like a god, even if they don't realize it?

Take Action

Find a coin in your house. Look at it closely. Most coins have a picture of a leader on them to show who has authority. This week, every time you see a coin, remember that God is the ultimate authority. He is the only King over your life and the whole world.

"The Big Idea"

God is one God, but He exists in three Persons: the Father, the Son, and the Holy Spirit.

SCRIPTURE FOCUS

"Therefore go and make disciples of all nations, baptizing them in the name of the Father and of the Son and of the Holy Spirit," - Matthew 28:19

The Great Mystery

Have you ever tried to think about how big space is? Or how many grains of sand are on every beach in the world? Your brain starts to feel a little bit "full," doesn't it? That is because some things are just bigger than our human minds can totally grasp.

The Trinity is the biggest mystery of all. In Systematic Theology, we use the word **Trinity** to describe how God is. It comes from "tri," meaning three, and "unity," meaning one. We believe in one God (as we learned last week), but that one God has three Persons: God the Father, God the Son (Jesus), and God the Holy Spirit.

They aren't three separate gods. And they aren't just three different "masks" that one God wears. They are three distinct Persons who have always loved each other and worked together.

How Can Three Be One?

It is hard to find a perfect example of the Trinity because nothing else in the world is exactly like God. But think about a musical chord. To play a C-major chord on a piano, you press three different notes: C, E, and G.

- ☐ If you play just one, it's a note.
- ☐ If you play all three together, it is still **one** chord.
- ☐ Each note is different, but they blend perfectly to make one sound.

The Father, Son, and Holy Spirit are like that. They are in perfect harmony. The Father plans, the Son obeys and saves us, and the Holy Spirit lives in us and helps us. They never argue, and they never disagree. They have been a "team" since before the world began.

Why the Trinity Matters to You

Because God is a Trinity, it means that God is **love**. Think about that. To have love, you need someone to love! Because God has always been Father, Son, and Holy Spirit, He has been practicing love forever. He didn't need to create humans because He was lonely. He created us so we could join in the love He already had!

When you are baptized "in the name" of the Father, Son, and Holy Spirit, you are being welcomed into that family. You aren't just following a set of rules; you are getting to know a God who is a perfect community of love. You have a Father who watches over you, a Savior (the Son) who is your brother and King, and a Spirit who is your constant helper.

Talk It Over

1. If God were just one person all by Himself before the world was made, do you think He would know how to love? Why or why not?

2. Which "Person" of the Trinity do you think about the most when you pray?

3. Why is it okay that we can't fully explain how the Trinity works with our human brains?

Take Action

Find a three-leaf clover or draw a triangle. Look at how there are three distinct parts, but it is still just one object. Keep that drawing or clover in your Bible this week to remind you that God is Three-in-One.

"The Big Idea"

God knows everything that has ever happened, everything happening now, and everything that will happen.

SCRIPTURE FOCUS

"Before a word is on my tongue you, Lord, know it completely." - Psalm 139:4

The Super-Computer of the Universe

Imagine you had a computer that knew the answer to every question in the world. It knew exactly how many fish were in the ocean. It knew the name of every star in every galaxy. It even knew what you were going to have for breakfast three years from today. That would be a pretty amazing machine, right?

God is much greater than any computer. In Systematic Theology, we use a big word for this: **Omniscience**. "Omni" means all, and "science" comes from a word meaning knowledge. So, God is "All-Knowing."

He doesn't have to study or look things up on the internet. He never says, "Wait, let me think about that," or "I didn't see that coming!" God has never learned a new fact in His entire life because He already knows everything there is to know.

He Knows the "Inside" You

Most people only see what you do on the outside. They see you play soccer, they see you do your chores, and they hear the words you say. But God sees what is happening on the inside.

He knows why you were sad this morning, even if you didn't tell anyone. He knows that you were trying to be brave when you were nervous about your math test. He even knows the words you are about to say before you even open your mouth!

This might sound a little bit scary at first. You might think, "Oh no, God knows when I have a mean thought!" And that's true. But here is the amazing part: Even though God knows every single mistake you've made and every bad thought you've had, He still loves you more than anyone else does. He knows the "real" you, and He still chooses to be your friend.

Why This Helps You Sleep at Night

Because God knows everything, He is never surprised by bad news. If a surprise storm happens or a plan goes wrong, God isn't worried. He already saw it coming, and He already has a plan to take care of you.

You don't have to explain your problems to God to "catch Him up" on the news. You can just talk to Him. You can say, "God, You know how I'm feeling," and He truly does. You can lean on Him because He has all the information. He knows the best way through every problem you will ever face.

Talk It Over

1. If you knew everything that was going to happen tomorrow, would you change anything about today?

2. Does it make you feel better or worse to know that God knows your thoughts? Why?

3. How does God's "all-knowing" power help Him be a better judge and king?

Take Action

Sit quietly for one minute. Think about one thing that has been worrying you lately. Now, tell God, "I'm glad You already know about this." Trust that because He knows the end of the story, He can help you with the page you are on right now.

God is not stuck in one place; He is present everywhere at the same time.

SCRIPTURE FOCUS

"Where can I go from your Spirit? Where can I flee from your presence?" - Psalm 139:7

The God Who Is Already There

Have you ever wished you could be in two places at once? Maybe you have a basketball game at the same time as your best friend's birthday party. Or maybe you are at school, but you really wish you were home on the couch. As humans, we can only be in one spot at a time. If you are in the kitchen, you aren't in the backyard.

God is different. In Systematic Theology, we use the word **Omnipresence**. "Omni" means all, and "presence" means being there. God is "All-Present."

This doesn't mean God is everything (God is not the grass or the TV). It means that there is no place in the entire universe where God is not. He is at the bottom of the deepest, darkest ocean where the glowing fish swim. He is on the far side of the moon. And He is right there in the room with you while you read this book.

No "No-God" Zones

Sometimes we think of God as only being at church. We walk into the building, sit in the pews, and think, "Okay, now I'm with God." But when we leave and go to the grocery store or the park, God doesn't stay behind in the church building.

King David, who wrote the verse for this week, realized that he could never run away from God. He said that if he flew to the highest clouds, God was there. If he hid in the darkest valley, God was there too. Even the darkness is like bright daylight to God.

This is amazing news because it means you are never, ever alone. If you feel lonely at school, God is at your desk. If you are scared in the middle of the night, God is right by your bed. You don't have to shout to get His attention because He is already closer than your own breath.

Why This Gives You Peace

Knowing God is everywhere changes how we act. If you knew a world-famous hero was standing right next to you, you would probably act your best! Knowing God is with us helps us make good choices even when no other people are watching.

But even more than that, His presence gives us rest. You don't have to go on a long journey to find God. You don't have to climb a mountain to get His help. Because He is everywhere, His power and His love are always available to you. You can talk to Him anywhere—on the bus, on the field, or in your room—and know that the King of the universe is listening.

Talk It Over

1. If you went to the moon, would you have to bring God with you, or would He already be there?

2. Does knowing God is always with you make you feel braver when you are in a dark room?

3. How does it change the way you pray to know that God is right next to you?

Take Action

Find a small object that you can carry in your pocket this week, like a smooth stone or a coin. Every time you touch it, let it be a reminder: "God is right here with me." Use it to remind yourself to talk to Him throughout the day about the small things, like a cool bird you saw or a funny joke you heard.

The Big Idea

God has the power to do anything that can be done; nothing is too hard for Him.

Scripture Focus

"Is anything too hard for the Lord? I will return to you at the appointed time next year, and Sarah will have a son."

– Genesis 18:14

The Power Without a Battery

Think about the strongest thing you have ever seen. Maybe it was a giant crane lifting a heavy truck, or a massive rocket blasting off into space. Those things have a lot of power, but they eventually run out of fuel. Batteries die, engines need gas, and even the strongest athletes get tired and need to sleep.

God never runs out of "juice." In Systematic Theology, we use the word **Omnipotence**. "Omni" means all, and "potence" means power (like the word "potent"). God is "All-Powerful."

Most powerful people have to work hard to get things done. If a king wants to build a castle, he has to hire thousands of workers and wait for years. But when God wanted to make the entire universe, He didn't use hammers or shovels. He simply spoke. He said, "Let there be light," and light appeared at thousands of miles per second. His voice is more powerful than a billion nuclear bombs, yet He can also use that power to hold a tiny sparrow in His hand.

What Does "Anything" Mean?

Does being all-powerful mean God can do literally anything? Well, there are some things God cannot do. He cannot lie. He cannot be mean. He cannot stop being God.

This is because God's power always works with His character. He only does things that are good and right. He is like a super-strong lighthouse. A lighthouse has enough power to shine through the thickest fog and the biggest waves, but its job is always to guide ships home safely. God uses His unmatched strength to take care of His creation and to keep His promises to you.

Why This Helps You When You Feel Weak

There will be days when you feel like you aren't strong enough. Maybe you have a project that feels too big, or a problem in your family that you can't fix. It is okay to be small. You don't have to have all the strength because you belong to the One who does.

When the Bible asks, "Is anything too hard for the Lord?" the answer is a giant **NO**. No heart is too hard for Him to change. No mistake is too big for Him to forgive. No storm is too loud for Him to quiet. When you are tired, you can "plug in" to His strength through prayer. You aren't just relying on your own muscles; you are relying on the arms that hold up the stars.

Talk It Over

1. If you had the power to change one thing in the world with just your words, what would it be?

2. Why is it a good thing that God cannot use His power to do something evil?

3. How does knowing God is all-powerful help you when you are afraid of something?

Take Action

Find something heavy in your house (that is safe to lift), like a big book or a gallon of milk. Lift it up and feel your muscles working. Think about how long you could hold it before your arm got tired. Then, remember that God holds the whole world in His hands and He never gets tired. Thank Him for being your strength today.

The Big Idea

God is perfectly pure, completely good, and unlike anyone or anything else.

SCRIPTURE FOCUS

"And they were calling to one another: "Holy, holy, holy is the Lord Almighty; the whole earth is full of his glory." - Isaiah 6:3

The Brightest White

Have you ever looked at a brand-new notebook or a fresh pile of snow? It looks so clean and bright. But if you put a regular white t-shirt next to that snow, the shirt might actually look a little gray or yellow. The snow shows you what "true" white really looks like.

In Systematic Theology, when we say God is **Holy**, we mean two things. First, it means He is "set apart." He is in a category all by Himself. He is not just a "better version" of a human; He is completely different and much higher than we are. Second, it means He is perfectly pure. There is not a single "speck" of sin, meanness, or wrong in Him. He is like a light so bright that it swallows up every shadow.

The "Triple" Holy

In the Bible, when someone wanted to say something was really important, they would repeat the word. If they said God was "Holy," that was great. If they said He was "Holy, Holy," that was huge. But in the verse for this week, the angels in heaven cry out, **"Holy, Holy, Holy."** This is the only quality of God that is repeated three times like this. It is His most famous trait. It means He is the "holiest of holy." Because He is three-times holy, He cannot even look at sin. He is so good that evil cannot stay in His presence. It would be like a tiny ice cube trying to sit on the surface of the sun—it just wouldn't work!

Why Holiness is Good News

Sometimes people think "holy" means "boring" or "strict." But think about it this way: Would you want to live in a world where the King was sometimes mean? Or a world where the Judge sometimes lied? That would be terrifying.

Because God is holy, we can trust Him completely. He will never trick you. He will never break a promise. He will never change His mind about what is right. His holiness is the reason we can feel safe with Him. He is the "Solid Truth" we talked about in Week 2. When we worship Him, we aren't just saying He is strong; we are saying He is perfectly, beautifully good.

1. If you had to pick a color to represent "Holy," what color would it be and why?

2. Why does the Bible repeat the word "Holy" three times instead of just once?

3. How does knowing God is perfectly good make you feel about following His rules?

Take Action

Find a piece of white paper. Try to find something else in your house that you thought was white, but actually looks a little "off-white" when you hold it next to the paper. Let that remind you that God's goodness is the standard for everything else. This week, when you pray, start by saying, "God, You are holy and good."

God is the perfect Judge; He always does what is right and treats everyone fairly.

"He is the Rock, his works are perfect, and all his ways are just. A faithful God who does no wrong, upright and just is he."

- Deuteronomy 32:4

The Umpire Who Never Misses

Have you ever played a game where the referee or umpire made a really bad call? Maybe you were clearly "safe" at home plate, but the umpire called you "out." It feels frustrating and unfair. It makes you want to stop playing because the rules don't seem to matter if the person in charge isn't getting it right.

In Systematic Theology, we call this the **Justice** or **Righteousness** of God. It means that God is the only Judge in the universe who never, ever makes a mistake. He doesn't have "favorites." He doesn't get distracted. He knows exactly what happened, why it happened, and what the right consequence should be.

Why Fairness Requires a Penalty

Imagine if a judge in a real courtroom let a person go free even though they had stolen someone's car. You wouldn't call that judge "kind." You would call that judge "unfair." To be a good and fair judge, you have to punish what is wrong and protect what is right.

Because God is just, He cannot simply "ignore" sin. If He ignored the bad things people do, He wouldn't be a good God. He would be like that umpire who doesn't care about the rules. This is why the Bible says God is a "God of truth and without iniquity." Iniquity is just a big word for sin. There is zero unfairness in Him.

The Great Solution

This creates a bit of a problem for us, doesn't it? If God is perfectly fair and must punish every wrong thing, and we have all done wrong things, what happens to us?

This is where the beauty of the Gospel comes in. God is perfectly **Just**, but He is also perfectly **Loving**. He didn't just ignore our sins; He sent Jesus to take the "penalty" for us. Imagine you broke a window and the judge said the fine was 100 dollars. You don't have the money. But then, the Judge Himself steps down from the bench, pulls out 100 dollars, and pays the fine for you. The law is satisfied (the fine was paid), but you go free. That is how God's fairness and love work together.

1. Why is it important for a judge to be "just and right" instead of just "nice"?

2. How does it make you feel to know that God sees when you are treated unfairly by others?

3. If God always does what is right, can we ever complain that He is being "mean" to us?

Draw a pair of balancing scales on a piece of paper. On one side, write "Wrong Choices." On the other side, write "The Price Paid by Jesus." Look at how they balance out. This week, when you see someone being treated unfairly at school or on a team, remember that God is the final Judge who will eventually make everything right.

"The Big Idea"

God does not just "have" love; He is love, and His love for you never ends.

SCRIPTURE FOCUS

"Whoever does not love does not know God, because God is love." - 1 John 4:8

More Than a Feeling

Have you ever used the word "love" to describe how you feel about pizza? Or maybe you "love" a new video game or a pair of sneakers. In our world, we use the word love to talk about things that make us feel good. But if the pizza gets cold or the sneakers get dirty, we might stop "loving" them pretty quickly.

God's love is not like that. In Systematic Theology, we learn that love is one of God's "attributes." That is a fancy word for a personality trait. But the Bible goes even further. It says God **is** love. It is the very core of who He is. Every single thing God does, even when He is being a fair Judge or a strong King, is done out of love.

Love Before the World Began

Remember back in Week 7 when we talked about the Trinity? This is where the Trinity becomes really important. Because God has always been three Persons (Father, Son, and Holy Spirit), He has been loving someone forever. Before there were any planets, any angels, or any people, the Father was loving the Son, and the Son was loving the Father.

God didn't create you because He was lonely and needed someone to love Him. He was already perfectly happy! He created you so that you could experience the amazing love He already had. It's like a happy family inviting a new friend over for a giant feast. They don't need the friend to bring food; they just want the friend to enjoy the party with them.

A Love That Does Not Quit

Sometimes we worry that if we make a big mistake, God will stop loving us. We think we have to "earn" His love by being perfect. But you can't earn something that is given as a gift.

In the Bible, there is a special word for God's love: **Hesed**. It is a Hebrew word that means "faithful, never-ending, promise-keeping love." It is the kind of love that stays even when things get hard. God's love is not based on how good you are today; it is based on how good He is. He loved you before you were born, He loves you right now, and He will love you billions of years from now. You can "soak" in that love like you soak in the warm sun at the beach.

1. What is the difference between "loving" a cheeseburger and "loving" a person?

2. Why is it good news that God's love doesn't depend on how well we behave?

3. If God is love, why do you think He sometimes tells us "no" to things we want?

Take Action

Find a sponge and a bowl of water. Put the dry sponge in the water and watch how it drinks up every drop until it is full. This week, every time you feel stressed or sad, imagine your heart is that sponge and you are soaking in God's love. Take a deep breath and say, "God, thank You for loving me just because I'm yours."

God never changes; His character, His power, and His promises are the same yesterday, today, and forever.

"I the Lord do not change. So you, the descendants of Jacob, are not destroyed." - Malachi 3:6

The Anchor in the Waves

Have you ever played at the beach and tried to build a giant sandcastle right where the waves hit the shore? It looks amazing for a few minutes. But then, the tide comes in. The water moves the sand, the walls melt away, and soon, your castle is gone. The beach is always changing. The sand moves, the water rises, and even the weather can turn from sunny to rainy in a heartbeat.

The world we live in is a lot like that beach. Your height changes every year. Your favorite food might change from pizza to tacos. Even your best friends might move away to a different city. It can be exhausting to keep up with a world that never stays still.

But God is like a massive, solid mountain of granite rising up behind that beach. The waves can hit it all they want, but the mountain doesn't move an inch. In Systematic Theology, we use a big word for this: **Immutability**. It just means "not able to change."

No "Bad Days" for God

Think about how you feel when you haven't had enough sleep or when you are really hungry. You might be a little grumpier than usual. Your "character" changes based on how you feel.

God never has a bad day. He never gets tired, so He never gets grumpy. He never learns something new that makes Him change His mind about you. If God was good a thousand years ago, He is exactly that good right now. If He hated lying when the Ten Commandments were written, He still hates lying today. You never have to wake up and wonder, "Which version of God am I going to get today?" He is the Unchanging One.

A Promise You Can Keep

The best part about God not changing is that His promises never "expire." If a friend promises to come over but then forgets, it's because humans are changeable. But when God makes a promise in the Bible, it is locked in forever.

Because He does not change, His love for you is "immutable" too. It isn't a "vibe" that comes and goes. It is a solid fact. When the world feels like it is spinning out of control and everything is changing too fast, you can reach out and hold onto God. He is the one part of your life that will be exactly the same when you are eighty years old as He is right now.

1. What is one thing about yourself that has changed since you were five years old?

2. Why would it be scary if God changed His mind about what is right and wrong?

3. How does knowing God stays the same help you trust Him when your life feels messy?

Find a large, heavy rock outside. Try to push it. Notice how it stays put. This week, whenever you feel nervous about a change, like a new grade at school or a move, remember that God is your Rock. Say to yourself, "The world changes, but my God stays the same."

Part 3:
Why Are We Here?
(Anthropology)

Now we move from studying God to studying people. In theology, this is called Anthropology. It isn't just about bones and history; it is about what it means to be a human being and why God decided to create us in the first place.

"The Big Idea"

You are special because God created you to reflect His own character.

"SCRIPTURE FOCUS"

"So God created mankind in his own image, in the image of God he created them; male and female he created them."

– Genesis 1:27

The Mirror of the King

Have you ever seen a master woodcarver or a painter finish a piece of art? Often, they will sign their name in the corner. But God did something even more amazing with you. He didn't just sign your name; He made you to be a "mirror" of Himself.

In Systematic Theology, we call this the **Imago Dei**. That is Latin for "Image of God." While God made the majestic lions and the giant redwood trees, He didn't make them in His image. Only humans have this special honor. Being made in God's image doesn't mean we look like Him physically (since God is a Spirit). It means our souls are built to reflect Him.

What is the "Image"?

Think about the things you can do that animals cannot. You can think about the future. You can write a poem or tell a joke. You can decide to be kind even when you are feeling grumpy. You can know the difference between right and wrong.

These abilities are like tiny sparks of God's own personality.

- **Creativity: God created the world; you create stories, drawings, or new games.**

- **Language: God spoke the world into being; you use words to encourage and help others.**

- **Justice: God is a fair Judge; you feel it in your heart when something isn't fair.**

Because you carry this "image," you have incredible value. It doesn't matter how fast you can run, how good your grades are, or what you look like. You have worth because of who made you.

Treating Others as Image-Bearers

Knowing that every person is made in the image of God changes how we treat people. The kid who sits alone at lunch is an image-bearer. The person who is hard to get along with is an image-bearer. Even people on the other side of the world who speak a different language carry the Maker's image.

When we are mean to others, we are actually being disrespectful to the Artist who made them. But when we show respect and kindness to every person, we are honoring God. You are a living, breathing masterpiece, and so is everyone else you meet today.

1. What is one thing humans can do that shows we are different from animals?

2. Does knowing you are made in God's image make you feel more confident? Why?

3. How should "Imago Dei" change the way you act when you see someone being bullied?

Take Action

Look in a mirror today. Instead of looking for messy hair or a smudge on your face, think: "I am looking at someone God created in His own image." Then, try to find one thing to compliment about a sibling or a friend, recognizing that God made them special too.

God put humans in charge of the world, not to use it up, but to take care of it for Him.

"The Lord God took the man and put him in the Garden of Eden to work it and take care of it." - Genesis 2:15

The King's Gardeners

Imagine your neighbor is going on a long trip. They have a beautiful backyard filled with rare flowers, a vegetable garden, and a birdbath. They hand you the keys and ask you to watch over it. They don't say, "Go ahead and pull up all the plants." They say, "Keep it healthy." They trust you to water the soil and make sure the birds have food. You are now the "manager" of that garden.

In Systematic Theology, we call this **Stewardship**. A steward is someone who takes care of something that belongs to someone else. The Bible tells us that "The earth is the Lord's," but He gave us the job of managing it. We are like the King's gardeners. From the very beginning, God gave humans the job to "dress" (work) and "keep" (guard) the earth.

Not the Boss, But the Guardian

Some people think that being "in charge" of the earth means we can do whatever we want. They think we can waste water, litter, or hurt animals just because we are humans. But that isn't what a good steward does. A good manager wants the owner to be happy when they return.

Because we are made in God's image, we should care for nature the way He does. God notices every sparrow that falls. He clothes the lilies of the field in beautiful colors. If the Creator cares about a tiny flower or a small bird, we should too!

Taking care of the earth is a way of saying "Thank You" to God for the home He built for us. When we plant a tree, recycle our plastic, or treat an animal with kindness, we are doing the work God gave us in the very first chapter of the Bible.

Why Science and Faith Work Together

This is where science gets really exciting for Christians. Biologists, foresters, and oceanographers are all people who study how the "garden" works. By learning about how bees pollinate flowers or how the ocean stays clean, we learn how to be better stewards.

God designed a perfect system where everything works together. Our job is to make sure we don't break that system. Whether you grow a small plant on your windowsill or help clean up a local park, you are fulfilling your purpose as a human being.

Talk It Over

1. If you were the owner of a beautiful forest, how would you feel if people left trash everywhere?

2. What is one way your family can be better "stewards" of the things God has given you?

3. Do you think God is pleased when we learn about how animals and plants work? Why?

Take Action

This week, do one "Stewardship Task." You could pick up three pieces of trash you see outside, water a thirsty plant, or make sure the lights are turned off when you leave a room to save energy. As you do it, say, "Lord, thank You for this world. Help me take good care of it."

"The Big Idea"

God gave us the power to make choices, and our choices matter to Him.

"SCRIPTURE FOCUS"

:"This day I call the heavens and the earth as witnesses against you that I have set before you life and death, blessings and curses. Now choose life, so that you and your children may live." - Deuteronomy 30:19

The Steering Wheel

Imagine you are sitting in the driver's seat of a go-kart. You have a steering wheel in your hands. You can turn left toward the grassy field, or you can turn right toward the paved track. The go-kart doesn't decide where to go on its own; you are the one making the decision.

In Systematic Theology, we call this **Moral Agency**. This is a big way of saying that God gave humans the ability to choose between right and wrong. We aren't like robots that only do what they are programmed to do. And we aren't like animals that only follow their instincts (like a hungry cat that eats a fish simply because it's there). God gave us a "steering wheel" for our lives.

The Gift of Choice

Why didn't God just make us into robots who always do the right thing? Well, think about your friends. Would you want a robot friend who was programmed to say "I like you" every five minutes? Probably not. You want a friend who chooses to be kind to you because they actually love you.

God wanted a real relationship with us. For love to be real, there has to be a choice. God gave us the freedom to choose to love Him and follow His ways, or to turn away and go our own way. This freedom is part of being made in His image. Because God is free, He made us free too.

Every Choice is a Seed

Every time you make a decision, it's like planting a seed. If you choose to tell the truth even when it's hard, you are planting a "blessing" seed. If you choose to be mean or dishonest, you are planting a "cursing" or "death" seed. Eventually, those seeds grow into a harvest.

Choosing the right way isn't always the easiest path. Sometimes the "wrong" turn looks like it might be faster or more fun. But God, our Great Designer, tells us to "choose life." He knows that when we use our steering wheel to follow His map, we find the most joy and the most safety.

Our choices have power—they can bring light to the people around us or they can bring darkness.

1. If you were a robot and had to do everything your parents said perfectly, would you still be "you"?

2. What is a hard choice you had to make recently? How did you feel after you made it?

3. Why do you think God lets us make mistakes instead of stopping us every time we try to do something wrong?

Today, every time you come to a "choice point" (like deciding what to say to a sibling or whether to finish your homework), stop for three seconds. Imagine you are holding a steering wheel. Ask yourself: "Which way leads to life?" Then, make the choice that honors God.

Part 4:

What Went Wrong?

(Hamartiology)

We now enter a part of our journey that is a bit like a detective story. We know the world is beautiful and that humans are special, but we also know that things aren't perfect. In theology, the study of sin and what went wrong is called Hamartiology.

Sin began when humans stopped trusting God's words and started listening to a lie.

SCRIPTURE FOCUS

"Now the serpent was more crafty than any of the wild animals the Lord God had made. He said to the woman, "Did God really say, 'You must not eat from any tree in the garden'?" - Genesis 3:1

The Poisoned Gift

Imagine someone gives you a beautiful, delicious-looking chocolate bar. But as you are about to take a bite, a stranger whispers, "Don't eat that. The person who gave it to you is trying to keep you from getting super-powers. If you eat a different one from *my* bag, you'll be like a superhero."

The stranger is lying, but if you believe him, you stop trusting your friend who gave you the gift. You start to think your friend is holding out on you. That is exactly what happened in the Garden of Eden.

God gave Adam and Eve a whole world of "Yes." They could eat from almost every tree, run through the fields, and talk with God. There was only one "No", the Tree of the Knowledge of Good and Evil. God didn't give that rule because He was mean; He gave it to protect them, like a parent telling a child not to touch a hot stove.

The Question Mark

The serpent (Satan) didn't start by yelling at Eve. He started by asking a sneaky question: *"Did God really say...?"* He wanted Eve to put a question mark where God had put a period.

The first lie wasn't just about fruit. The lie was that **God is not good.** The serpent made Eve believe that God was hiding something wonderful from her and that she would be better off being her own boss. This is the root of all sin: deciding that we know better than God and that we don't need to trust His heart.

The Fall

When Adam and Eve ate the fruit, something broke. In theology, we call this **The Fall**. It wasn't just a mistake; it was a rebellion. By choosing to listen to the lie instead of the Truth, they walked away from the light and into the shadows.

Every lie we tell today, every time we are selfish, and every time we disobey, it usually starts with that same old question: "Is God's way really the best way?" When we spot the lie, we can choose to hold onto the truth instead.

1. Why do you think the serpent used a question instead of just telling Eve to eat the fruit?

2. Have you ever felt like God's rules were "keeping you" from having fun? Was that a truth or a lie?

3. What is the difference between a "mistake" (like dropping a glass) and "sin" (like choosing to lie about who broke it)?

Take Action

Find a piece of paper and draw a big question mark. On one side of the question mark, write a lie (like "God doesn't care about me"). On the other side, write the truth from the Bible (like "God loves me"). This week, when you feel tempted to do something wrong, ask yourself: "Am I listening to a lie or the Truth?"

"The Big Idea"

Sin isn't just something we do; it's a "sickness" of the heart that affects every human being.

"SCRIPTURE FOCUS"

"For all have sinned and fall short of the glory of God," - Romans 3:23

The Smudged Lens

Imagine you are wearing a pair of glasses, but they are covered in greasy fingerprints and dust. No matter where you look, at a beautiful sunset, a math book, or your best friend's face, everything looks a little bit blurry and messy. It isn't the world that's blurry; it's the lenses you are looking through.

In Systematic Theology, we call this **Original Sin** or **Total Depravity**. That second one sounds like a scary term, but it doesn't mean that every person is as mean as they could possibly be. It just means that sin has "smudged" every part of us: our thoughts, our feelings, and our choices. Because we are related to Adam and Eve, we are born with a heart that naturally wants to go its own way instead of God's way.

The "Missing the Mark" Problem

The Bible uses a specific word for sin that comes from archery. Imagine an archer aiming at a target. If the arrow hits the bullseye, that is perfection. If the arrow misses by an inch, or if it misses by a mile, it still "missed the mark."

God's "mark" is His perfect holiness (remember Week 11?). Because God is perfect, even our "small" sins, like a tiny white lie or a grumpy attitude, mean we have missed the mark. The verse for this week says we "come short." It's like trying to jump across a giant canyon. It doesn't matter if you jump five feet or fifty feet; if you don't reach the other side, you fall. We all fall short of God's perfection.

Why Admitting It Is a Good Thing

Admitting we are sinners might feel sad at first, but it is actually the beginning of the best news ever. Think about a person who is sick but doesn't know it. They won't go to the doctor, and they won't get the medicine they need. But the moment they admit, "I am sick," they can start to get help.

When we admit the truth, that we can't be perfect on our own, we stop trying to "save ourselves." We realize we need a Savior. Admitting the truth doesn't make God love you less; it actually opens the door for Him to show you His amazing grace. He already knows the truth about our hearts, and He is just waiting for us to agree with Him so He can start the healing.

Talk It Over

1. Why is it easier to notice when other people miss the mark than when we miss it ourselves?

2. If everyone has sinned, does that mean sin "doesn't matter," or does it mean we all need the same help?

3. How does it feel to know that you don't have to pretend to be perfect around God?

Take Action

Find a white piece of paper and make a small pencil smudge in the middle. Try to erase it completely. Usually, you can still see a tiny mark where the smudge was. This week, when you make a mistake or act selfishly, don't try to hide it or blame someone else. Instead, say, "God, I missed the mark. Thank You for loving me anyway and for being the only One who can clean my heart."

"The Big Idea"

Sin didn't just change people; it broke the harmony of the whole world.

SCRIPTURE FOCUS

"We know that the whole creation has been groaning as in the pains of childbirth right up to the present time." - Romans 8:22

The Out-of-Tune Piano

Have you ever heard a piano that hasn't been tuned in a long time? When you press a key, it doesn't sound quite right. It might be too high or too flat. Even if a world-famous musician sits down to play a beautiful song, it will still sound "off" because the instrument itself is broken.

When Adam and Eve sinned, it was like the whole world went "out of tune." In Systematic Theology, we call this the **Curse**.

God's original design was perfect, no thorns, no sickness, no hurricanes, and no animals hurting each other. But because humans were the "kings and queens" of the earth (remember Week 16?), when we fell into sin, the whole "kingdom" fell with us.

Thorns and Tumbleweeds

Before the Fall, work was easy and fun. But after sin entered the world, God told Adam that the ground would produce thorns and thistles. Work would become hard and sweaty.

This explains why the world can be so confusing today. We see a beautiful sunset, but then we hear about a scary earthquake. We see a cute puppy, but then it gets sick. The world is still God's masterpiece, but it's a masterpiece that has been damaged. It's like a beautiful painting with a coffee stain on it. The beauty is still there, but so is the "groaning."

The Hope of a New Song

If the story ended here, it would be very sad. But the same Bible that tells us the world is broken also tells us that God is a Master Repairman.

Just like a piano tuner can tighten the strings and make the music beautiful again, God has a plan to fix the whole world. The Bible promises that one day, there will be a "New Heaven and a New Earth." The thorns will be gone, sickness will vanish, and even the lions and lambs will be friends again.

When you see something broken in the world today—like a wilted flower or a stormy day—it should remind you that this isn't how things are supposed to be. It should make us look forward to the day when God makes everything "in tune" once more.

1. What is something in nature that you think is beautiful? What is something in nature that can be scary?

2. Why do you think God let the earth be affected by our sin?

3. How does it change the way you feel about "bad things" (like getting a cold) when you know God plans to fix the world one day?

Take Action

Go outside and look for a weed or a prickly thorn. Carefully look at it and remember that these weren't in the original Garden. Then, find a beautiful flower or a green leaf. Thank God that His beauty is still visible even in a broken world, and ask Him to help you look forward to His "New Creation."

Part 5:
Who Is Jesus?
(Christology)

Now we reach the most exciting part of our journey! We've seen that God is holy and that humans have "missed the mark," leaving the world broken. Christology is the study of Jesus Christ, the One who came to fix the break and bring us back to God.

"The Big Idea"

Jesus is not just a good man; He is God Himself who became a human to live among us.

"SCRIPTURE FOCUS"

In the beginning was the Word, and the Word was with God, and the Word was God." - John 1:1

The King in Disguise

Imagine a powerful King who lives in a beautiful, golden palace. He hears that the people in a small, poor village are suffering from a sickness. Instead of just sending a letter or a servant, the King takes off his crown, puts on the simple clothes of a villager, and moves into a small house right in the middle of the town. He eats their food, walks their dusty roads, and feels their pain so that He can heal them from the inside out.

This is what Jesus did. In Systematic Theology, we use a big word for this: **The Incarnation**. "In" means in, and "carnis" means flesh (like "chili con carne"). It means God "put on skin."

Jesus didn't start existing when He was born in Bethlehem. As "The Word," He has always existed with God the Father. But He chose to become a tiny baby, to get sleepy, to get hungry, and to grow up just like you, all while still being 100% God.

Why the "Word"?

Have you ever had a thought in your head that you couldn't quite explain until you spoke it out loud? Words help us understand what someone is thinking. The Bible calls Jesus "The Word" because He is God's way of "speaking" to us. If you want to know what God is like, how He feels about you, or how He wants you to live, you just have to look at Jesus. He is the perfect "translation" of God into human language.

Two Natures, One Person

This is one of the coolest mysteries in theology: Jesus is **fully God** and **fully man** at the exact same time.

- Because He is **Man**, He can represent us and understand what it feels like to be sad, tired, or tempted.
- Because He is **God**, He has the power to save us and forgive our sins.

He is the "Bridge" between Heaven and Earth. He didn't stay far away in the clouds; He moved into our neighborhood to show us the way home.

1. If you could ask God one question, what would it be? (Hint: Looking at Jesus' life might give you the answer!)

2. Why was it important for Jesus to feel things like hunger and tiredness just like we do?

3. How does it make you feel to know that the God who made the stars once slept in a wooden manger?

Take Action

Find a glove. Put your hand inside of it. The glove moves and acts because your hand is inside it, but your hand and the glove are two different things. This week, let that remind you of the Incarnation: how God (the hand) "dwelt inside" human flesh (the glove) to reach us. Every time you see your own hands, thank Jesus for becoming a human for you.

"The Big Idea"

Jesus is the perfect sacrifice who took the weight of the world's mess so we wouldn't have to.

"SCRIPTURE FOCUS"

"The next day John saw Jesus coming toward him and said, "Look, the Lamb of God, who takes away the sin of the world!"
- John 1:29

The Debt We Couldn't Pay

Imagine you were exploring a museum and accidentally knocked over a glass case holding a diamond worth millions of dollars. The alarm goes off, the guards come running, and you realize there is absolutely no way you could ever pay for what was broken. You have a debt that is simply too big for your piggy bank.

In the old days of the Bible, people felt this way about their sin. They knew that "missing the mark" (what we call sin) created a gap between them and God. To show they were sorry and to "cover" that debt, they would bring a perfect, spotless lamb as a sacrifice. The lamb took the person's place. It was a serious, heavy reminder of how much sin costs. But those lambs were only temporary. They were like using a small band-aid on a giant wound—they helped for a moment, but they couldn't truly heal the heart for good.

The Ultimate Trade

When John the Baptist saw Jesus walking toward the river one morning, he shouted something that probably surprised everyone: **"Behold the Lamb of God!"** John wasn't saying Jesus looked like a farm animal. He was telling the crowd that the "Final Sacrifice" had finally arrived. In theology, we call this the **Atonement**. If you break the word down, it looks like **At-One-Ment**. It's the act of making us "at one" with God again. Because Jesus never sinned, He was the only person in history who was "spotless." He didn't have any debt of His own, so He could offer to pay ours.

Why a Lamb?

Think about how gentle a lamb is. It doesn't growl or fight back. When people were mean to Jesus, He didn't use His "Omnipotence" to zap them or prove He was stronger. Instead, He chose to be quiet and brave. He laid down His life on purpose.

It's as if the Son of the Museum Owner walked into the room while you were crying over the broken glass and said, "Don't worry. Put the bill on my account. I'll pay for it all." Because of

Jesus, our "sin debt" is marked *Paid in Full.* We don't have to hide from God or worry that He's holding our mistakes against us. The Lamb has taken them away.

1. If you were a superhero, would it be harder to fight a villain or to let someone be mean to you without fighting back? Why did Jesus choose the second way?

2. What does it mean to be a "substitute"? (Like when a teammate fills in for you in a game).

3. How does it change your day to know that God isn't "keeping score" of your mistakes anymore?

Find something soft and white today, maybe a fluffy towel or a cotton ball. As you feel how soft it is, remember that Jesus is the "Gentle Lamb." Think of one thing you feel bad about doing this week, and then imagine Jesus taking that "bill" and throwing it away. Thank Him for being your substitute.

"The Big Idea"

Jesus didn't just tell us how to live; He showed us a completely new way to see the world.

SCRIPTURE FOCUS

"When Jesus had finished saying these things, the crowds were amazed at his teaching, because he taught as one who had authority, and not as their teachers of the law."

- Matthew 7:28-29

The Teacher Who Sat on the Grass

Imagine you go to school, and instead of a teacher standing at a whiteboard with a boring textbook, your teacher takes the whole class out to a beautiful hillside. He points at the wildflowers and tells you how much God cares about them.

He tells stories about sneaky farmers, lost coins, and a son who ran away from home.

When Jesus started His ministry, people were used to teachers who just listed out long, dusty rules. But Jesus was different. He was the **Great Teacher**. In theology, we call this His **Prophetic Office**. A prophet is someone who speaks the truth of God to people.

Jesus didn't just repeat what others said. He spoke like He was the one who wrote the rules. He would say, "You have heard it said... but I say to you..." He wasn't just giving more homework; He was showing us the heart of God.

Upside-Down Kingdom

Jesus taught something very strange. He taught that in God's kingdom, everything is "upside-down" compared to how the world works.

- In the world, the strongest people are the most important. But Jesus said, **"Blessed are the humble."**

- In the world, you should be mean to people who are mean to you. But Jesus said, **"Love your enemies."**

- In the world, having lots of toys makes you "rich." But Jesus said that being kind and generous is the real way to be wealthy.

He used stories called **Parables**. These were simple stories with big, hidden meanings. He used them so that people who really wanted to know God could understand, while people who were just being nosy would be confused.

Why We Listen

We don't listen to Jesus just because His ideas are nice. We listen because He is the "Word" we talked about in Week 21.

If the person who designed the entire universe tells you how life works best, it's probably a good idea to pay attention!

Jesus' teaching isn't about trying harder to be a "good kid." It's about changing the way we think. He taught us that God doesn't just want us to follow rules on the outside; He wants our hearts to be full of love on the inside. When we listen to Him, we aren't just learning facts, we are learning how to be truly alive.

Talk It Over

1. If you could sit on the grass and listen to Jesus tell one story, what would you want it to be about?

2. Why is "loving your enemies" a lot harder than just following a rule like "don't steal"?

3. What do you think Jesus meant when He said the last will be first and the first will be last?

Take Action

Pick one of Jesus' "Upside-Down" rules today. For example, if someone is mean to you at school, instead of being mean back, try to say something kind or just pray for them. Notice how it feels to follow the Great Teacher's way instead of the world's way.

Jesus' miracles were like "trailers" for a movie, showing us that He has the power to fix everything sin has broken.

"Then will the eyes of the blind be opened and the ears of the deaf unstopped. Then will the lame leap like a deer, and the mute tongue shout for joy. Water will gush forth in the wilderness and streams in the desert." (Isaiah 35:5-6)

The Fingerprints of the Creator

Have you ever seen a movie trailer? It's a short video that shows you the best parts of a movie that hasn't come out yet. It gives you a "sneak peek" of what the whole story will be like.

When Jesus was on earth, He did amazing things that no one else could do. He calmed a roaring storm with three words ("Peace, be still"). He turned a small lunch of bread and fish into a feast for thousands. He even made people who were sick or couldn't walk perfectly healthy again. In theology, we call these **Miracles**.

Jesus didn't perform miracles just to "show off" or act like a magician. His miracles were "sneak peeks" of what the world will look like when He finishes fixing it. Every time He healed someone, He was saying, "In My Kingdom, there will be no more pain." Every time He calmed the sea, He was saying, "In My Kingdom, nature will be at peace again."

Power Over the Brokenness

Remember back in Week 20 when we talked about the "Broken World"? Sin brought sickness, hunger, and scary storms. Because Jesus is the one who made the world in the first place, He has the authority to tell those broken things to "be fixed."

- **Nature: He walked on water because He is the Master of the waves.**
- **Sickness: He touched people that everyone else was afraid of and made them clean.**
- **Death: He even called His friend Lazarus out of a grave, showing that not even death can stand in His way.**

These miracles prove that Jesus is who He says He is. Only the Architect of the building knows how to fix the walls when they crack. Jesus' miracles were like His "ID card," proving to everyone that the King had arrived.

Sometimes we wonder why Jesus doesn't perform a miracle for every problem we have right now. While He still hears our prayers and can do anything, the miracles He did in the Bible were meant to point us to something even bigger: the healing of our souls.

The greatest miracle isn't just a sick body getting well; it's a heart that was far from God coming home. Jesus showed us He has the power to change the weather and heal the skin, which means we can trust Him to have the power to change our hearts, too.

Talk It Over

1. If you could have seen one of Jesus' miracles in person, which one would you pick?

2. Why is it important that Jesus didn't just *talk* about being God, but actually showed it through His power?

3. How does knowing Jesus can calm a storm help you when you feel "stormy" or scared on the inside?

Take Action

Go to your kitchen and look at some bread or a piece of fruit. Think about how Jesus could take something that small and feed thousands of people. This week, when you face a "big" problem that feels too hard for you, remember the Miracle Worker. Say to yourself: "Nothing is too big for the One who can calm the sea."

" The Big Idea "

On the cross, Jesus took the punishment we deserved so we could have the friendship with God we didn't earn.

" SCRIPTURE FOCUS "

"But God demonstrates his own love for us in this: While we were still sinners, Christ died for us." - Romans 5:8

The Great Exchange

Imagine you are standing in a courtroom. You've been caught red-handed doing something wrong, and the judge says the fine is a million dollars. You don't have it. You're about to be led away when suddenly, the Judge's own Son walks to the front. He takes off his royal robe, stands where you are standing, and hands over the money. He takes your spot, and you are told you can go home free.

In theology, we call this **Substitutionary Atonement**. That's a mouthful, but "Substitution" just means one person taking the place of another. On the cross, a "Great Exchange" happened. Jesus took our "mess", our lies, our selfishness, and our rebellion, and gave us His "perfection" instead.

Why Did He Have to Die?

It's a sad and heavy question. Why couldn't God just say, "It's okay, I forgive you," without the cross?

Remember Week 12? God is perfectly **Just**. He can't just ignore wrong things, or He wouldn't be a good Judge. But God is also perfectly **Loving**. The cross is where God's Justice and His Love met. He didn't ignore the sin; He paid for it Himself. He didn't want us to be punished, so He took the "blow" for us.

The Power of "It is Finished"

When Jesus was on the cross, His very last words were, "It is finished." In those days, when a person paid off a debt at a store, the shopkeeper would write those same words on the receipt. It meant the bill was paid in full. There was nothing left to owe.

The cross wasn't a defeat; it was a victory. It was the moment Jesus defeated the power of the "First Lie" from Week 18. He showed once and for all that God is not holding out on us, He is actually giving us everything, including His own life. Because of the cross, the "No Entry" sign between us and God has been torn down forever.

Talk It Over

1. If someone did something wrong to you, is it easier to punish them or to forgive them and take the hurt yourself?

2. Why is it important that Jesus stayed on the cross even though He had the power to come down?

3. What does "It is Finished" mean for the mistakes you might make tomorrow?

Find two sticks or two pencils and lay them across each other to make a cross. Look at them and think about the "Great Exchange." Say out loud: "Jesus, You took my place so I could be Your friend." This week, whenever you feel "not good enough," remember that Jesus' perfect record is now yours.

"The Big Idea"

Jesus didn't stay dead! His resurrection proves He is the King of Life and that death has been defeated.

"SCRIPTURE FOCUS

"He is not here; he has risen, just as he said. Come and see the place where he lay." - Matthew 28:6

The Surprise Ending

Imagine reading a book where the hero gets defeated in the middle of the story. It feels like the "bad guys" have won and the light has gone out. You're about to close the book in sadness, but then you turn the page and find out the hero had a secret plan all along. He wasn't defeated, He was just getting ready for the greatest comeback in history.

Early on Sunday morning, three days after Jesus died, His friends went to the tomb expecting to find a body. Instead, they found a giant stone rolled away and a bright angel sitting there with a smile. The tomb was empty. In theology, we call this the **Resurrection.**

Why the Empty Tomb Matters

The Resurrection is the most important event in Systematic Theology. If Jesus had stayed in the grave, He would have just been a good teacher who died a sad death. But by walking out of the tomb, He proved three massive things:

1. **He is God:** Only the Author of Life has the power to take His life back up again.

2. **The Price was Accepted:** The empty tomb is God the Father's way of saying, "The payment Jesus made on the cross worked!"

3. **Death is Defeated:** Death is like a giant "predator" that has caught every human being in history. But Jesus was too "big" for death to hold. He broke the teeth of death so that we don't have to be afraid of it anymore.

A Real Body

Jesus wasn't a ghost when He came back. He ate fish with His friends. He let them touch the scars on His hands. He had a real, physical body, but it was a *new* kind of body. It was a "Glorified Body" that would never get sick, never age, and never die again.

Because Jesus rose from the dead, we have a "Living Hope." It means that for those who follow Him, death isn't the end of the story, it's just a doorway to a new, better life. The same power that brought Jesus out of the grave is the power that lives inside us today!

1. How do you think the disciples felt when they saw the empty tomb for the first time?

2. Why is it better that Jesus rose with a real body instead of just being a spirit or a ghost?

3. How does knowing Jesus is alive right now change how you talk to Him when you pray?

Take Action

Find a seed (like a sunflower seed or a bean) or even a small pebble. Hold it in your hand and think about how something that looks "dead" and dry can burst into a living plant when it's put in the ground. This week, every time you see a flower or a green plant, say, "Jesus is alive, and He makes all things new!"

"The Big Idea"

Jesus went back to heaven to prepare a place for us, but He is coming back one day to finish His rescue mission and reign as King.

SCRIPTURE FOCUS

"And if J go and prepare a place for you, J will come back and take you to be with me that you also may be where J am."

- John 14:3

The Promise to Return

Imagine your favorite person in the whole world, maybe a parent or a grandparent, has to go away on a long trip. Before they leave, they give you a big hug and say, "I'm going to get everything ready for you, and then I'm coming back to get you so we can be together forever." Even though you miss them while they are gone, you live every day with a little bit of excitement, watching the door and waiting for their return.

After Jesus rose from the dead, He spent forty days with His friends before He went up into heaven. In theology, we call this the **Ascension**. But as He was leaving, He made a massive promise: He is coming back.

What is He Doing Now?

Right now, Jesus isn't just "taking a break" in heaven. He is busy!

- **He is Preparing:** He told us He is getting a place ready for us. Think of it like the most amazing home you can imagine, built by the Creator of the stars.

- **He is Praying:** He is talking to God the Father about *you* right now, cheering you on and helping you.

- **He is Ruling:** Even though we can't see Him, He is already the King of the universe, making sure everything happens according to His good plan.

The Grand Finale

The first time Jesus came, He came quietly as a baby in a manger. But the Bible says the next time He comes, it will be very different. He won't be a humble lamb; He will be the **Returning King**.

When He returns, He will fix every broken thing we talked about in Week 20. He will wipe away every tear. There will be no more mean people, no more sickness, and no more "missing the mark." He will finally set up His Kingdom of Love where everyone lives in peace. We don't know the exact day or hour He will arrive, but we live "on tip-toe," ready and excited for His return.

1. If Jesus came back today, what is the first thing you would want to show Him or tell Him?

2. How does it change the way you act today if you know the King might walk through the door at any moment?

3. Why is it good news that Jesus is in heaven praying for us right now?

Take Action

Find a window in your house that looks out at the sky. Spend one minute looking at the clouds and remembering that Jesus is coming back. This week, whenever you see something sad or unfair in the world, say to yourself, "It's okay; the King is coming back to fix this."

Part 6:
How Are We Saved?
(Soteriology)

We've seen the problem (sin) and the Person who fixed it (Jesus). Now, we look at how that rescue mission actually reaches us. In theology, this is called Soteriology— the study of how God saves people and brings them into His family.

You don't have to work to earn God's love; you just have to receive the gift He is already offering.

"For it is by grace you have been saved, through faith—and this is not from yourselves, it is the gift of God— 9 not by works, so that no one can boast." - Ephesians 2:8-9

The Birthday Party Rule

Imagine it's your birthday. Your best friend walks in with a huge box wrapped in bright paper and a big bow. They hand it to you and say, "Happy Birthday!"

Now, imagine if you reached into your pocket, pulled out five dollars, and tried to pay them for the gift. Or what if you said,

"Wait! Before I open this, let me go mow your lawn and wash your car so I deserve it." That would be silly, right? It wouldn't be a gift anymore—it would be a paycheck.

In Systematic Theology, we call this **Grace**. Grace is getting something wonderful that you didn't earn and don't deserve. God doesn't wait for us to be "good enough" before He saves us. He offers us the gift of being His friend simply because He is generous.

Faith is the "Hand"

If a gift is sitting on a table in front of you, it doesn't do you any good until you reach out and take it. In the Bible, reaching out to take God's gift is called **Faith**.

Faith isn't just knowing facts about Jesus. Even the "bad guys" in the Bible knew facts about Him! Faith is **Trust**. It's like sitting down in a chair. You don't just "believe" the chair will hold you; you actually put your weight on it. When we have faith, we are "putting our weight" on the fact that Jesus paid our debt on the cross.

No Room for Boasting

The verse for this week says that salvation is not "of works." That means you can't get to heaven by being 10% better than your neighbor or by collecting enough "good deed points."

Why did God do it this way? Because if we could earn it, we would spend all our time bragging about how great we are. "Look at me! I'm so holy that God had to let me in!" But because it's a free gift, all we can do is say "Thank You." It keeps us humble and it keeps our eyes on the Giver, not on ourselves.

1. Why is it sometimes hard to accept a gift without trying to "pay" for it or earn it?

2. What is the difference between *knowing* a chair can hold you and actually *sitting* in it?

3. If salvation is a free gift, does that mean it wasn't expensive? (Think back to Week 25!)

Take Action

Find an empty box and wrap it in some scrap paper or put a ribbon on it. Put it somewhere you can see it this week. Every time you see that "gift," remember that God's love and forgiveness are free for you. You don't have to be perfect today to be loved by Him. Just say, "Thank You, God, for Your amazing grace."

Repentance is more than just feeling bad; it's making a U-turn in your heart to head in God's direction.

"Repent, then, and turn to God, so that your sins may be wiped out, that times of refreshing may come from the Lord,"
- Acts 3:19

The GPS "Recalculating"

Have you ever been in a car when the GPS says, "In 500 feet, make a U-turn"? It usually happens because the driver missed a turn or started heading the wrong way. The GPS doesn't just yell, "You're doing it wrong!" It gives you a way to get back on the right path.

In Systematic Theology, we call this **Repentance**. The Greek word used in the Bible is metanoia, which literally means "a change of mind." It's like you were walking toward a dark, scary forest (sin), but you suddenly realize, "Wait, this isn't where I want to be!" So, you stop, turn your whole body around, and start walking toward the sunshine (God).

Two Sides of One Coin

You can't really have the "Free Gift" of Faith (from Week 28) without Repentance. They are like two sides of the same gold coin.

- **Faith is turning** *toward* **Jesus.**

- **Repentance is turning away from your own way.**

Imagine you are holding a handful of dirty rocks and someone offers you a handful of diamonds. To take the diamonds, you have to let go of the rocks. Repentance is simply letting go of the "dirty rocks" of our sin so we can grab onto the "diamonds" of God's grace.

It's Not Just "I'm Sorry"

There is a big difference between being sorry you got caught and being sorry you did the wrong thing. If a person says "sorry" for stealing a cookie but plans to steal another one as soon as you leave the room, they haven't repented. They just have a "sad feeling."

True repentance means you agree with God that your way was a "missed mark" and you truly want to change. It's a happy thing, not a scary one! The Bible says repentance leads to "times of refreshing." It's like taking a cool shower after a long, sweaty day. You feel clean, light, and ready to move forward.

1. Why do you think it's hard for us to admit when we are going the wrong way?

2. Can you think of a time when you said "sorry" but didn't actually mean you were going to stop? How did that feel different from a time you really changed?

3. If God already knows our mistakes, why is it important for us to tell Him we are turning around?

Take Action

Find a spot in your house where you have enough room to walk. Start walking in one direction, and then shout, "Metanoia!" and do a fast U-turn to walk the other way. This week, when you find yourself being selfish or unkind, picture that U-turn in your head. Tell God, "I'm changing my mind about this," and start walking His way again.

" The Big Idea "

God doesn't just "pardon" us like a judge; He welcomes us into His home as His very own children.

SCRIPTURE FOCUS

"The Spirit you received does not make you slaves, so that you live in fear again; rather, the Spirit you received brought about your adoption to sonship. And by him we cry, "Abba, Father." - Romans 8:15

From the Courtroom to the Living Room

Imagine you were in a lot of trouble, the kind of trouble where you're standing in a courtroom (remember Week 25?). The judge clears your name and says, "You're free to go." That would be amazing, right? You'd be relieved. But then, imagine the judge stands up, walks over to you, gives you a hug, and says, "I don't want you to just go home. I want you to come home with *me*. I'm making you my son (or daughter). Everything I have is now yours."

In Systematic Theology, we call this **Adoption**. Most of the time, we think of "being saved" as just getting a "Get Out of Jail Free" card. But God goes way further. He doesn't just want to be your Judge or your Creator; He wants to be your **Father.**

"Abba" – The Secret Word

The Bible uses a very special word for God: Abba. It's an Aramaic word that is a lot like saying "Papa" or "Daddy." In the ancient world, you would never call a king or a high official by such a close, personal name. It would be considered disrespectful.

But because of what Jesus did, God gives us permission to use that kind of "family talk" with Him. We don't have to walk on eggshells or act like we're talking to a scary boss. We can come to Him with our scraped knees, our bad days, and our big dreams, knowing He's listening like a loving dad.

The Royal Inheritance

When you are adopted into a family, you get the family name and the family "stuff." The Bible says we are "heirs of God." That means everything that belongs to Jesus, His peace, His joy, and His eternal home, belongs to us, too.

You aren't a guest in God's house; you're a member of the family. This means you don't have to "perform" to keep your spot. Your parents don't kick you out of the family because you forgot to clean your room or got a bad grade; they love you because you're *theirs*. God is the same way, only even better.

1. What is the difference between a "servant" and a "child"? How does a servant act around the master compared to how a child acts around a father?

2. Why is it cool that we can call the Creator of the Universe "Abba"?

3. How does it change your day to know that you are a "Royal Heir"?

Write your name on a piece of paper. Underneath your name, write: **"Child of the King."** Put it on your mirror or inside a notebook. This week, whenever you feel lonely or like you aren't "good enough," look at that paper and remember that you have been adopted into the biggest, best family in existence.

Being saved isn't like a game of "tag" where you're in one minute and out the next. God is the one who holds onto you, and He never lets go.

"I give them eternal life, and they shall never perish; no one will snatch them out of my hand." - John 10:28

The Parent's Grip

Imagine you are walking through a massive, crowded theme park with your dad. It's loud, there are thousands of people, and it would be really easy to get lost. You are holding onto his hand as tight as you can. But here's the secret: your dad isn't just waiting for you to hold on, he has his big, strong hand wrapped firmly around *yours*.

If you get distracted by a cool toy or a shiny sign and accidentally loosen your grip, do you disappear? No! Because your dad is the one doing the heavy lifting. He's the one making sure you don't get lost.

In Systematic Theology, we call this **Eternal Security** or the **Perseverance of the Saints**. It's a fancy way of saying that because God started the work of saving you (Week 28), He is responsible for finishing it. Your safety doesn't depend on how tightly you can hold onto God; it depends on how tightly He is holding onto you.

The Double-Hand Protection

Jesus took this idea even further. He said that we are in *His* hand, and then He said His hand is inside God the Father's hand.

Think about that! To "lose" your salvation, someone would have to be stronger than Jesus and God the Father combined. Since God is **Omnipotent** (remember Week 13?), that's impossible. You are tucked away in the safest "double-grip" in the universe.

What About My Mistakes?

Does this mean we can just go out and be mean or move back into the "Scary Forest" from Week 29? Of course not! When you know someone loves you that much and is keeping you that safe, you want to stay close to them.

When we mess up, we might feel "out of sync" with God, like a radio that has some static. We might need to "Recalculate" our path, but we don't stop being His child. A mistake might break your *closeness* for a moment, but it never breaks your *relationship*. You are part of the family forever.

1. Have you ever been worried that God was "done with you" because you made a mistake? How does Jesus' "hand" promise change that?

2. Why is it better that God is the one keeping us saved instead of us having to do it ourselves?

3. If you knew you were 100% safe and could never be "kicked out" of God's family, how does that make you want to live?

Take Action

Trace your hand on a piece of paper. Inside that hand, draw a tiny stick figure of yourself. Then, draw another, bigger hand traced around the first one. This is your "Double-Grip" reminder. Hang it up somewhere to remind you that even on your "bad" days, you are tucked safely inside God's power.

Salvation isn't just about where you go when you die; it's about who you are becoming while you live.

"Therefore, if anyone is in Christ, the new creation has come: The old has gone, the new is here!" - 2 Corinthians 5:17

The Extreme Home Makeover

Imagine a house that has been abandoned for years. The windows are broken, the roof leaks, and the garden is full of weeds. Then, a new owner buys it. The moment they sign the papers, the house belongs to them. That's like **Justification**: God legally declares you His.

But the new owner doesn't just leave the house messy. They move in and start working. They fix the plumbing, paint the walls a bright color, and plant flowers in the yard. Day by day, the house starts to look different.

In Systematic Theology, we call this **Sanctification**. It's the lifelong process of God the Holy Spirit changing us from the inside out so that we start to think, talk, and act more like Jesus.

Fruit, Not Just Rules

A lot of people think being a "new person" means trying really hard to follow a long list of "Do's and Don'ts." But think about an apple tree. Does the tree wake up in the morning and scream, "I have to work hard to grow an apple today!"? No. If the tree is healthy and connected to the soil, the apples just grow naturally.

When you stay connected to God, He grows "fruit" in your life. The Bible calls these the **Fruit of the Spirit**: love, joy, peace, patience, kindness, goodness, faithfulness, gentleness, and self-control. You'll notice that as you grow, you might find it easier to be kind to someone who was mean to you, or you might feel a strange sense of peace even when things are going wrong. That's not just you "being a good kid"—that's God renovating His house!

The "Already but Not Yet"

Here is the tricky part: even though you are a "new creature," you still have moments where you act like the "old you." You might still lose your temper or tell a lie. Does that mean the renovation failed?

Not at all! Sanctification is a journey, not a sprint. We are "already" saved, but we are "not yet" perfect. God is a patient builder. He doesn't get mad that the house isn't finished on the first day; He just keeps working on the next room. The goal isn't to be perfect tomorrow; it's to be a little bit more like Jesus today than you were yesterday.

1. Can you think of one way you've changed since you started learning about God? (Maybe you're more patient or you pray more?)

2. Which "Fruit of the Spirit" do you think you need the most help with right now?

3. Why is it good news that God is the one doing the "renovating" instead of us having to do it all by ourselves?

Find a small seed or a bean. This week, keep it in your pocket. Every time you touch it, remember that God has planted a "New Person" seed inside you. It might look small now, but with God's help, it is growing into something beautiful. When you have a hard moment, ask God: "What room in my heart are we working on today?"

Part 7:

Who Is the Holy Spirit?

(Pneumatology)

Welcome to Part 7! We've talked about God the Father (the Creator) and God the Son (the Savior). Now, we meet the third person of the Trinity: the Holy Spirit. In theology, this study is called Pneumatology. The word comes from the Greek pneuma, which means "breath" or "wind."

" The Big Idea "

The Holy Spirit is God's invisible but powerful presence living inside everyone who follows Jesus.

SCRIPTURE FOCUS

"And I will ask the Father, and he will give you another advocate to help you and be with you forever— the Spirit of truth. The world cannot accept him, because it neither sees him nor knows him. But you know him, for he lives with you and will be in you." - John 14:16-17

The Invisible Power

Imagine you are standing on a beach. You can't see the wind. You can't reach out and grab a handful of it, it doesn't have a color, and it doesn't show up in photos. But you know it's there. You see the palm trees bending, you feel the cool breeze on your face, and you watch kites fly high. You know the wind is real because you can see what it **does**.

The Holy Spirit is a lot like that. In Systematic Theology, we call this study **Pneumatology**. The word comes from the Greek *pneuma*, which means "breath" or "wind." While Jesus walked on earth where people could see Him, the Holy Spirit works "under the radar." He is God's very breath. When Jesus went back to heaven, He didn't leave us to figure things out alone; He sent the Spirit to be our "Comforter" or "Helper."

Not a "Force," but a "Friend"

Sometimes people talk about the Holy Spirit like He's just a "vibe" or a battery. But the Bible is clear: the Holy Spirit is a **Person**.

- He has feelings: **The Bible says we can make Him sad (grieve Him) when we are mean to others.**

- He has a mind: **He knows the deep thoughts of God and explains them to us.**

- He has a will: **He chooses how to help us and what gifts to give us.**

The coolest part? When Jesus was on earth, He could only be in one place at a time. If He was in one town, He wasn't in the next. But the Holy Spirit is everywhere at once! He lives *inside* every believer. That means God isn't just "up there" or "out there": He is as close to you as your own breathing.

The Power Source

Think of a high-tech drone. It has cameras, propellers, and a sleek design. But if the battery is dead, it's just a fancy paperweight. It needs power to get off the ground.

The Holy Spirit is like the "power" for our lives. He gives us the strength to do things that are normally really hard, like being brave when we're scared, telling the truth when it's awkward, or being kind when someone is getting on our nerves. He "recharges" our hearts so we can live the way Jesus showed us.

Talk It Over

1. If you can't see the Holy Spirit, how can you tell He is working in someone's life? (What are the "bending trees" you might see?)

2. Why do you think Jesus called the Spirit a "Comforter"? When do you feel like you need a "Helper" the most?

3. How does it change your day to think that the Creator of the universe is literally living *inside* you right now?

Take Action

Take a deep breath in through your nose and blow it out slowly. As you breathe in, think: *"God, thank You for Your Spirit."* As you breathe out, think: *"Help me feel Your power today."* Do this three times. This week, whenever you feel overwhelmed or lonely, remember that the "Breath of God" is right there with you.

The Holy Spirit gives every believer a unique "superpower" designed to help the whole church family grow.

SCRIPTURE FOCUS

"There are different kinds of gifts, but the same Spirit distributes them. There are different kinds of service, but the same Lord. There are different kinds of working, but in all of them and in everyone it is the same God at work. Now to each one the manifestation of the Spirit is given for the common good." - 1 Corinthians 12:4-7

The Swiss Army Knife Problem

Imagine you're out on a camping trip. You need to saw a branch, open a can of beans, and tighten a loose screw on your flashlight. If you only had a spoon, you'd be in for a very frustrating night. You need different tools for different jobs.

In theology, we call these **Spiritual Gifts**. When the Holy Spirit lives in you, He doesn't just sit there: He brings a "toolbox." But here's the catch: He doesn't give every tool to one person. If you were a "Swiss Army Knife" who could do everything perfectly, you'd never need anyone else. God wants us to need each other, so He sprinkles different gifts across the whole group.

Talent vs. Gift: What's the Difference?

You might already be great at drawing, soccer, or math. Those are natural talents, and they are awesome! But a Spiritual Gift is a bit different. It's a special ability the Spirit activates in you specifically to show people who God is.

- **A Talent might be having a great singing voice that makes people clap.**

- **A Spiritual Gift might be using that voice (or even a shaky one!) to help people feel God's peace when they are sad.**

Common gifts include things like **teaching** (making hard things easy to understand), **encouragement** (being a "cheerleader" for people's souls), **giving** (being super generous), or **mercy** (really feeling for people who are hurting).

You Are a Body Part

The Bible says the church is like a human body. Think about how ridiculous it would be if your body was just one giant eyeball. You'd see everything, but you couldn't walk, eat, or high-five anyone.

The Holy Spirit made you a specific "part."

- ☐ Maybe you're the **hand** that helps clean up.
- ☐ Maybe you're the **mouth** that speaks up for someone being bullied.
- ☐ Maybe you're the **feet** that go out of your way to visit someone who is lonely.

When you find your "special talent" and use it, the whole "body" stays healthy. You aren't just a spectator; you're a vital part of the team.

1. What is one thing you enjoy doing that makes other people feel happy or helped?

2. Why do you think it's better that we all have *different* gifts instead of everyone having the *same* one?

3. If you feel like you don't have a "gift" yet, does that mean the Holy Spirit missed you? (Spoiler: The Bible says he gives them to "every man", or person!)

This week, be a "Gift Detective." Instead of looking at yourself, look at your friends or family. When you see someone doing something helpful, like a sibling being really patient or a parent explaining something clearly, say to them: "I think that's one of your Spiritual Gifts!" Sometimes, other people see our "superpowers" before we do.

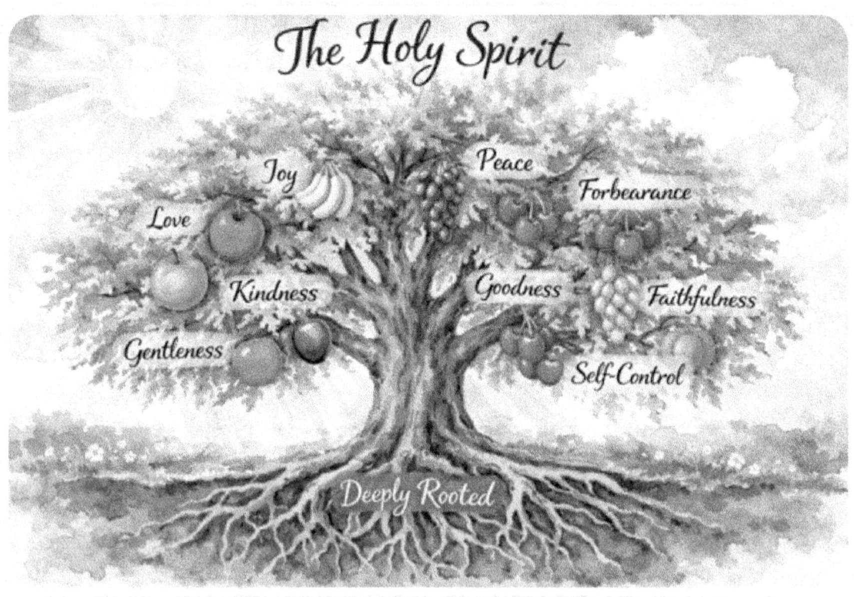

"The Big Idea"

Being a Christian isn't about following a checklist of rules; it's about letting the Holy Spirit grow a whole new personality inside you.

Scripture Focus

"But the fruit of the Spirit is love, joy, peace, forbearance, kindness, goodness, faithfulness, gentleness and self-control. Against such things there is no law." - Galatians 5:22-23

The "Taped-On" Apple

Imagine you have a dead, brown tree in your backyard. You really want it to be an apple tree, so you go to the grocery store, buy a bag of shiny red apples, and use duct tape to stick them onto the branches. From the street, it might look like a healthy tree. But as soon as a wind blows or a week passes, those apples are going to fall off and rot. Why? Because they aren't connected to the *life* of the tree.

A lot of people try to "tape on" good behavior. They try really hard to be "nice" or "patient" so they look like a good person. But in Systematic Theology, we learn that real change is a "Fruit," not a "Work." Fruit grows naturally when a tree is healthy and connected to the soil. When you stay connected to the Holy Spirit, these nine qualities start to grow from your heart to your hands.

The Nine-Flavor Harvest

The Bible lists nine specific "flavors" of fruit that the Holy Spirit produces. You don't get to pick and choose: He grows the whole "fruit basket" in you at once!

- **The Upward Fruit: Love, Joy, and Peace (These help us stay close to God).**
- **The Outward Fruit: Longsuffering (Patience), Gentleness, and Goodness (These help us get along with others).**
- **The Inward Fruit: Faith, Meekness (Gentleness), and Temperance (Self-control, this helps us manage our own big feelings).**

Character vs. Performance

Here's a secret: Spiritual Gifts (what we talked about last week) are about what you **do**. But the Fruit of the Spirit is about who you **are**.

You could have the "gift" of being a great speaker, but if you don't have the "fruit" of love, you're just making a lot of noise. The Holy Spirit is much more interested in your character than your "performance." He wants you to be the kind of person who is kind even when no one is watching, and peaceful even when things are going wrong.

1. Which of the nine fruits do you think is the "sweetest" or most helpful to have in your house right now?

2. Why is "self-control" (Temperance) considered a gift from God rather than just "trying harder"?

3. Have you ever seen someone who was really "talented" but wasn't very "kind"? How does that help us see why the Fruit is so important?

Take Action

Pick one "Fruit" from the list today. Let's say it's **Gentleness**. Every time you open a door, pet a dog, or speak to a sibling today, try to do it with "Holy Spirit Gentleness." At the end of the day, ask yourself: *Did I do that on my own, or did I ask the Helper for a little boost?*

"The Big Idea"

The Holy Spirit doesn't just give us a map and leave us to figure it out; He walks the path with us to help us make the right turns.

SCRIPTURE FOCUS

"But when he, the Spirit of truth, comes, he will guide you into all the truth. He will not speak on his own; he will speak only what he hears, and he will tell you what is yet to come." - John 16:13

The Compass in Your Heart

Have you ever been lost in a big store or on a hiking trail? It's a sinking feeling. You look around, and suddenly everything looks the same. You wish you had someone who knew the way to just grab your hand and lead you out.

In theology, we talk about the Holy Spirit's work of **Guidance**. Life is full of "Which way do I go?" moments. Should I be friends with this person? How do I handle this argument? What should I do when I grow up? The Holy Spirit is like a personal GPS for your soul. But unlike a phone GPS that sometimes loses its signal, the Spirit has a perfect "connection" to God's heart.

The Light on the Page

Sometimes, you read the Bible and it feels like a confusing, dusty old book. Then, suddenly, a verse you've read ten times before "pops" out at you. It's like someone turned a flashlight on in a dark room.

Theologians call this **Illumination**. The Holy Spirit is the one who "wrote" the Bible (by helping the human authors), so He is the best one to explain it! He helps you see how a story written thousands of years ago actually applies to the problem you're having at school today.

The "Nudge"

The Holy Spirit usually doesn't shout through a megaphone. Most of the time, His guidance feels like a "still, small voice" or a gentle nudge in your heart.

- It might be a sudden thought to go say something kind to a kid who looks lonely.
- It might be a "check" in your spirit; a feeling that says, *Wait, maybe I shouldn't press 'send' on that mean text.*
- It might be a sense of peace about a hard decision.

He doesn't force us to follow Him, but He is always whispering the best way to go. Our job is to learn how to turn down the "volume" of the world so we can hear Him.

1. Can you think of a time when you felt a "nudge" to do something good, even if you weren't sure why?

2. Why is it better to have a *Guide* who walks with us instead of just a *Rulebook* to follow by ourselves?

3. What makes it hard to hear the "still, small voice" of the Spirit when we are busy or upset?

Take Action

Practice the **"Five-Second Pause"** this week. Before you react when you're angry, or before you make a choice, stop for five seconds and just think: *"Holy Spirit, what do You want me to do?"* You don't have to wait for a lightning bolt; just look for that quiet sense of peace or that gentle nudge toward what is right.

Part 8: What Is the Church? (Ecclesiology)

We've spent a lot of time talking about who God is and how He saves us. Now, we look at the "team" He put together to represent Him on Earth. This is Ecclesiology. While many people think of a building with a steeple when they hear the word "church," theology shows us that the Church is actually a living, breathing group of people.

"The Big Idea"

The Church isn't a place you go; it's a family you belong to and a "Body" that works together.

SCRIPTURE FOCUS

"Now you are the body of Christ, and each one of you is a part of it." - 1 Corinthians 12:27

Not a Clubhouse, but a Living Thing

Imagine you see a hand lying on a table by itself. It's pretty creepy, right? A hand is only useful and "alive" when it's attached to an arm, which is attached to a shoulder, which is connected to a heart and a brain.

In the Bible, Jesus is called the "Head," and we are called His "Body." This means that the Church isn't just a club for people who like the same book; it's a living organism. When the "Head" (Jesus) wants to show love to someone, He uses His "hands" (us). When He wants to go somewhere to help, He uses His "feet" (us).

The Two Types of "Church"

Theologians usually talk about the Church in two ways:

- **The Universal Church: This includes every person who has ever trusted Jesus, all over the world, from the very beginning of time until now. It's a massive, invisible family that spans across every country and language. +1**

- **The Local Church: This is the specific group of people you meet with on Sundays or in your neighborhood. They are the "boots on the ground" who know your name, pray for you when you're sick, and help you grow.**

Why We Need the "Awkward" Parts

Have you ever noticed that the people in a church can be very different? Some are old, some are young, some are quiet, and some are loud. Sometimes, people in the church can even be a bit annoying!

But that's part of the plan. A body where every part was an eye would be a disaster. God puts different people together so we can learn to love folks who aren't exactly like us. We "build" the body by showing up and using our unique gifts (remember Week 34?) to make the whole group stronger.

Talk It Over

1. If Jesus is the "Head" of the body, what happens if the "hands" or "feet" decide they don't want to listen to Him?

2. What is the difference between going to church and being the church?

3. Why is it more powerful to help people as a group rather than just trying to do everything alone?

Take Action

Find a Lego set or a box of building blocks. Build something where every block is a different color or shape. Look at how they all have to lean on each other to stay up. This week, think of one way you can "support" someone in your local church family—maybe by writing a note of encouragement or helping clean up after a meeting.

"The Big Idea"

We don't just gather because it's a tradition; we gather because we are like coals in a fire: we stay "hot" for God much better when we are together.

"SCRIPTURE FOCUS"

"And let us consider how we may spur one another on toward love and good deeds, 25 not giving up meeting together, as some are in the habit of doing, but encouraging one another, and all the more as you see the Day approaching." - Hebrews 10:24-25

The Glowing Coal Analogy

Imagine you have a big, roaring campfire. In the center, there is a pile of bright red, glowing coals. If you take a pair of tongs, pick up one single coal, and set it on the cold dirt two feet away from the fire, what happens? Within a few minutes, that coal stops glowing. It turns grey, gets cold, and loses its heat.

But if you take that same cold, grey coal and toss it back into the pile with the others, it starts to glow red-hot again.

In Systematic Theology, we see that the Christian life was never meant to be a "solo sport." We are designed to live in **Community**. When we gather together, we "heat each other up" by sharing stories of what God is doing, praying for each other, and reminding each other of the truth.

What is Worship, Anyway?

Most people hear "worship" and think of singing songs. While singing is a huge part of it, the word actually comes from an old English word, worth-ship. It means to declare how much someone is **worth**.

When we gather for worship, we are doing three things:

1. Looking Up: **We tell God how great He is (Adoration).**
2. Looking In: **We check our hearts and ask for forgiveness (Confession).**
3. Looking Out: **We listen to the Bible so we know how to live in the world (Instruction).**

"Provoking" Each Other

The verse for this week uses a funny word: "provoke." Usually, we think of provoking as something bad, like a sibling poking you until you get mad. but the Bible says we should provoke each other to **love and good works**.

In the church family, we are supposed to be each other's biggest cheerleaders. When you see a friend at church being kind, you "provoke" them by saying, "I saw you do that, and it was awesome! Keep going!" We gather so that no one has to face the "Scary Forest" (from Week 29) alone.

1. Why is it harder to stay excited about God when you are all by yourself for a long time?

2. What is your favorite part of "gathering together"? Is it the music, the teaching, or just seeing your friends?

3. How can you "provoke" someone to do something good this week?

Take Action

This week, imagine you are a "heat seeker." Look for someone in your church or family who seems a little "grey" or discouraged (like the cold coal). Send them a quick text, write them a note, or give them a high-five. Just by being there for them, you are helping their fire stay lit.

Jesus gave us special "action-reminders" called Baptism and Communion to help us feel, see, and taste His love.

"and when he had given thanks, he broke it and said, "This is my body, which is for you; do this in remembrance of me.""

- 1 Corinthians 11:24

The Heavenly Souvenirs

Have you ever gone on a great vacation and bought a souvenir, like a seashell or a keychain, just so you wouldn't forget how much fun you had? Whenever you look at it, the memories come rushing back.

In Systematic Theology, we call these **Ordinances** (or sometimes Sacraments). They are specific things Jesus "ordered" us to do. He knew that we are humans who forget things easily, so He gave us two "souvenirs" that we don't just look at, but actually do.

1. Baptism: The Public Jersey

Imagine you've just joined the best team in the world. You're excited, but nobody knows you're on the team yet. Then, you put on the jersey. Now, everyone who sees you knows exactly who you belong to.

Baptism is like that jersey. When a person is dipped under the water and brought back up, they are acting out a "mini-movie" of Week 25 and 26:

- **Going under the water: Shows that our old, selfish self has died with Jesus.**

- **Coming up out of the water: Shows that we have been raised to a brand-new life! It's a way of saying to the whole world, "I'm with Jesus now."**

2. The Lord's Supper: The Holy Snack

The night before Jesus went to the cross, He sat down for a meal with His friends. He took bread and juice and said, "Every time you do this, think of Me."

We call this **Communion** or the **Lord's Supper**.

- **The Bread: Reminds us that His physical body was hurt for us.**

- **The Juice: Reminds us of His blood that "washes" our sins away.**

It isn't a meal to fill your stomach; it's a meal to fill your heart. When we eat it together at church, it reminds us that we are all equal at God's table. No matter who you are, we all need the same "Bread of Life."

1. Why do you think Jesus chose bread and juice as reminders instead of something fancy like gold or diamonds?

2. If Baptism is like a "mini-movie," what part of the movie is your favorite to watch?

3. How does eating a meal *together* help a church feel more like a family?

The next time you eat a piece of bread or a cracker, take a second before you chew. Look at it and think, *"Jesus, thank You for giving Your body for me."* This week, look for a "souvenir" of God's goodness in your life, maybe a photo of a fun time or a gift from a friend, and say a quick "thank you" to the One who gave it to you.

"The Big Idea"

The Church isn't a secret club; it's a group of messengers sent to share the best news in history with everyone, everywhere.

"SCRIPTURE FOCUS"

"Therefore go and make disciples of all nations, baptizing them in the name of the Father and of the Son and of the Holy Spirit," - Matthew 28:19

The Last Words

If you were going on a long trip and could only say one last thing to your family before you left, you'd probably choose something really important. You wouldn't say, "Don't forget to buy more milk." You'd say, "I love you," or "Take care of each other."

Before Jesus went back to heaven, His very last instructions to His friends were what we call **The Great Commission**. He told them that the "Rescue Mission" wasn't over just because He was leaving. Instead, the Church was now responsible for taking that message to the whole world.

What is the "Gospel"?

In theology, we use the word **Gospel** all the time. It's a Greek word (*euangelion*) that literally means **"Good News."** There is a big difference between advice and news.

- **Advice is someone telling you what you *should* do ("You should eat your vegetables").**

- **News is someone telling you what has already *happened* ("The war is over! We won!").**

The Church doesn't go around just giving people "good advice" on how to be nice. We go around telling "Good News", that Jesus has already defeated sin and death, and that anyone can be God's friend for free.

You Are a Witness

Sometimes, telling people about Jesus feels scary. We think we have to be "experts" or have all the answers to hard science questions. But Jesus didn't call us to be "lawyers"; He called us to be **Witnesses**.

In a courtroom, a witness doesn't have to know all the laws in the book. They just have to stand up and say, "This is what I saw, and this is what happened to me." You are a witness of God's love when you tell someone, "I used to be really scared, but God gave me peace," or "I know God loves me because He's been so kind to my family." You're just one beggar telling another beggar where to find bread.

1. If you found a cure for every disease in the world, would it be "mean" or "kind" to tell everyone about it? How is the Gospel like that?

2. Why is "Good News" easier to share than "Good Advice"?

3. Who is one person in your life who might need to hear some "Good News" today?

Take Action

Think of the "Good News" like a bright light. This week, try to "shine" by doing something unexpectedly kind for someone who doesn't go to your church. If they ask why you're being so nice, you can just say, "I'm practicing being like my friend, Jesus." You don't need a microphone to tell the Good News; sometimes you just need a helping hand.

Part 9:
How Should We Live?
(Christian Living)

Now that we understand who God is, what Jesus did, and how the Holy Spirit helps us, we get to the "practical" part. How does all this theology change the way we act on a Tuesday afternoon? This is often called Christian Ethics or Sanctification in Action. It's about taking the truth and putting legs on it.

" The Big Idea "

Prayer isn't a magical incantation or a formal speech; it's simply a child talking to a Father who actually enjoys listening.

SCRIPTURE FOCUS

"pray continually," - 1 Thessalonians 5:17

The Walkie-Talkie

Imagine you are an explorer in a deep, thick jungle. It's beautiful, but it's also easy to get lost or tripped up by vines. Luckily, you have a high-powered walkie-talkie clipped to your belt. On the other end of that radio is the Base Commander who has a satellite view of the whole forest. He can see the paths you can't see, and he has all the supplies you might need.

Prayer is that walkie-talkie. Many people think prayer is only for when you're in a church building or right before you eat a snack. But the Bible says to pray "without ceasing." That doesn't mean you have to keep your eyes closed all day (that would be dangerous while walking!), it means you keep the "radio" turned on. You can talk to God while you're doing math, playing soccer, or lying in bed.

The "A.C.T.S." Method

Sometimes we don't know what to say to God. If you feel stuck, theologians often use a simple "cheat sheet" called the A.C.T.S. model to help cover all the bases:

- **A - Adoration: Telling God how "awesome" He is. ("God, You made the stars, and they are incredible!")**

- **C - Confession: Admitting where we missed the mark. ("I'm sorry I was mean to my brother today.")**

- **T - Thanksgiving: Saying thank you for the good stuff. ("Thanks for the pizza and for my cool teacher.")**

- **S - Supplication: A fancy word for asking for help. ("Please help my grandma feel better.")**

Does He Always Answer?

If you asked your dad for a bowl of sharp nails for breakfast, he would say "No." Not because he's mean, but because he loves you!

God answers prayer in three ways: **Yes, No, or Wait.** * **Yes:** He gives us exactly what we asked for.

- **No: He has a better plan that we can't see yet.**

- **Wait: He is growing our patience because the timing isn't right.**

Because He is **Omniscient** (Week 13), He knows what we need before we even ask. Prayer isn't about changing God's mind; it's about changing our hearts to match His.

1. If God already knows everything, why do you think He still wants us to tell Him about our day?

2. Which part of "A.C.T.S." is the easiest for you? Which part is the hardest?

3. How would it change your day if you treated prayer like a "walkie-talkie" that was always on?

Pick a "Prayer Trigger" this week. Every time you walk through a door or every time you see the color red, say a tiny, one-sentence prayer. It could be as simple as, *"Help me be kind right now,"* or *"Thank You for this day."* See how many times you can "check in" with your Father today!

"The Big Idea"

Living for God is like being a well-trained athlete or a brave soldier; we have to practice saying "no" to things that pull us away from Him.

"Scripture Focus"

"Fight the good fight of the faith. Take hold of the eternal life to which you were called when you made your good confession in the presence of many witnesses." - 1 Timothy 6:12

The Training Ground

Imagine you want to run a marathon. You don't just wake up on Saturday morning and run 26 miles. If you tried that, your legs would turn to jelly! To win the race, you have to train. You have to say "no" to eating only candy and "yes" to waking up early to practice.

In theology, we call the struggle against wrong choices **Spiritual Warfare**. It sounds like a big, scary movie title, but it mostly happens in the small moments of your day. It's the "fight" that happens inside your head when you really want to say something mean back to someone who insulted you, or when you're tempted to take something that isn't yours.

The Three "Opponents"

In the "Good Fight," we usually face three different types of challenges:

1. The World: **The pressure to "fit in" and do what everyone else is doing, even if it's wrong.**

2. The Flesh: **That little voice inside us that just wants to be lazy, selfish, or the boss of everything.**

3. The Enemy: **The "First Liar" (from Week 18) who tries to trick us into thinking God's way is boring or mean.**

Putting on the Armor

God doesn't send you into the fight empty-handed. He gives you what the Bible calls the **Armor of God**. Each piece protects a different part of your heart and mind.

- **The Belt of Truth: Knowing what is actually true so you don't get tricked.**

- **The Breastplate of Righteousness: Protecting your heart by doing what is right.**

- **The Shield of Faith: Trusting God to stop the "scary thoughts" that come at you.**

- **The Sword of the Spirit: Using the Bible to remind yourself of God's promises.**

The goal isn't to be "tough" on your own. The goal is to stay close to the Commander. A soldier who stays close to the Captain is always the safest.

1. What is the hardest "fight" you usually have during the day? (Is it being patient, being honest, or being kind?)

2. Which piece of the "Armor of God" do you think you need to put on first when you wake up?

3. Why do you think the Bible calls it a "good" fight? (Hint: Think about what happens if we win!)

Take Action

Find an old belt, a hat, or even a pair of sturdy shoes. As you put them on tomorrow morning, imagine you are putting on your spiritual armor. Say to yourself: *"Today, I'm going to fight for kindness. I'm going to fight to be honest."* Remember, every time you choose to do the right thing when it's hard, you are winning a round in the "Good Fight."

"The Big Idea"

In God's Kingdom, the way to be "the best" is to be the best at serving others. It's a "backwards" kind of greatness.

SCRIPTURE FOCUS

"Do nothing out of selfish ambition or vain conceit. Rather, in humility value others above yourselves," - Philippians 2:3

The Upside-Down Kingdom

Imagine you are at a crowded birthday party. The cake is about to be served. In most places, everyone rushes to be first in line. The strongest or the fastest get the biggest pieces with the most frosting. We are taught that to be "Number One," you have to push past everyone else.

But Jesus taught something totally different. He lived in an **Upside-Down Kingdom**. He said that if you want to be the greatest, you should act like the person whose job it is to serve the meal and clean up the crumbs. He didn't just say it, He did it! Even though He was the King of the Universe, He spent His time washing His friends' dirty feet and helping people that everyone else ignored.

Moving "Me" to the Back

In theology, we call this **Humility**. Humility isn't thinking that you are "bad" or "ugly" or "talentless." It actually means **thinking of yourself less.** Think of a "Selfie" versus a "Group Photo."

- A **Selfie** is all about *my* face, my hair, and *my* smile.

- A **Group Photo** is about making sure everyone is in the frame, everyone is smiling, and the whole group looks good together.

Putting others first means looking at life like a group photo. Instead of asking, "How does this help me?" we start asking, "How can I make *their* day better?"

The Secret to Joy

Here is the strange thing about putting others first: it actually makes you happier! People who spend all their time trying to be "Number One" are usually very stressed out because they are always worried someone will overtake them.

But when you are busy looking for ways to help your mom with the dishes, or letting a friend pick the game you play, or listening when someone else is talking, you find a special kind of "Kingdom Joy." You realize that you don't have to carry the heavy crown of being the "most important." You can just enjoy being a helper in God's family.

1. Why is it so hard to let someone else go first? What are we afraid will happen?

2. Can you think of a time when someone put you first? How did it make you feel?

3. Does "putting others first" mean you have to let people be mean to you? (Hint: No! It means being kind and helpful, but still standing up for what is right.)

Take Action

This week, try to be a **"Secret Servant."** Look for one job at home that isn't yours, like picking up toys that aren't yours or clearing a plate, and do it without telling anyone. When you do it, whisper to yourself: *"This is for the Upside-Down Kingdom."* See if you can go the whole week without getting "caught" being helpful!

"The Big Idea"

Forgiveness isn't about saying what happened was "okay"; it's about letting go of the "debt" so your own heart doesn't stay heavy.

SCRIPTURE FOCUS

"Be kind and compassionate to one another, forgiving each other, just as in Christ God forgave you." - Ephesians 4:32

The Heavy Backpack

Imagine someone is mean to you at school. They say something rude or break something that belongs to you. It feels like they gave you a big, heavy rock. If you stay angry and plan how to get them back, it's like putting that rock in your backpack and carrying it everywhere you go.

After a while, your back starts to hurt. You can't run as fast, and you aren't as happy. The other person might not even know you're carrying that rock! In theology, we call this **Unforgiveness**. When we refuse to forgive, we aren't hurting the other person, we are weighing ourselves down.

The "Debt" Canceled

In the Bible times, forgiveness was often compared to money. If you owed someone 100 dollars and they "forgave" the debt, it meant you didn't have to pay them back.

Jesus told a famous story about a man who was forgiven a massive debt by a King (remember Week 25?). But then, that same man went out and grabbed a friend by the neck over a tiny amount of money. The King was sad because the man didn't understand that since he had been forgiven *so much*, he should be the first person to forgive others.

How Do We Do It?

Forgiving is one of the hardest things the Holy Spirit (Week 33) helps us do. Here is what forgiveness is **not**:

- ☐ It is **not** pretending it didn't happen.
- ☐ It is **not** saying, "It's fine!" (Because it wasn't fine).
- ☐ It is **not** trusting the person immediately if they are still being mean.

Forgiveness is simply saying: *"God, this person hurt me, but I'm giving the 'rock' to You. I'm not going to try to hurt them back. I'm letting go of the debt because You let go of mine."*

1. Why is it so tempting to want to "get even" when someone is mean to us?

2. How does remembering that God forgave us help us forgive someone else?

3. Does forgiving someone mean you have to be best friends with them right away? (Hint: You can forgive someone and still keep a safe distance until they show they have changed!)

Take Action

Find a physical rock outside. Hold it in your hand and think about someone you are upset with. Feel how heavy and hard the rock is. Then, say a prayer: *"God, I'm tired of carrying this. I forgive [Name], and I'm giving this to You."* Then, drop the rock! Every time you feel that anger coming back this week, remember that the rock is on the ground and you don't have to pick it up again.

"The Big Idea"

Bravery isn't the absence of fear; it's trusting that God is bigger than whatever is scaring you.

SCRIPTURE FOCUS

"When I am afraid, I put my trust in you." - Psalm 56:3

The Night-Light Promise

Have you ever been in a room that was so dark you couldn't see your own hand in front of your face? In the dark, ordinary things like a pile of clothes or a chair can look like scary monsters. Your heart beats fast, and you want to hide under the covers. But what happens when you turn on a light? You realize the "monster" was just your laundry, and you are actually safe.

In life, we go through "dark rooms", times when things get hard, someone we love gets sick, or we have to do something that makes us feel small and nervous. In theology, we call this **Trusting in Providence**. This is the belief that God is in control of the details of our lives, even when we can't see the "light" yet.

Courage is a Muscle

Most people think brave people don't feel scared. But that's a myth! If you aren't scared, you don't need bravery. Bravery is what happens when your knees are shaking but you decide to move forward anyway because you know God is walking right beside you.

Think of David and Goliath (from Week 21). David was a young boy facing a giant warrior. Do you think his heart was beating fast? Probably! But David looked at the giant and then he looked at God. He realized that compared to the Creator of the Universe, the giant was actually the small one. Being brave means keeping your eyes on the **Omnipotent** (All-Powerful) God instead of the problem.

The "Peace" Guard

The Bible says that when we are worried, we should talk to God about it, and He will give us a "peace that passes understanding." It's like a spiritual bodyguard that stands at the door of your heart and mind to keep the "scary thoughts" out.

You might still be in a hard situation, but inside, you feel a strange calmness. That's the Holy Spirit (The Helper) reminding you that the story isn't over and that God always wins in the end.

1. What is one thing that has made you feel scared lately?

2. If you knew for a fact that the strongest Person in the world was standing right behind you, how would that change how you feel about your "giant"?

3. Why does God tell us to "Fear not" so many times in the Bible? (Is it because life isn't scary, or because He is always there?)

Take Action

Find a flashlight or use the light on a phone. In a dark room, shine it at the wall. Notice how the light always "wins" against the dark. This week, whenever you feel a "dark" thought or a fear creep in, say out loud: **"God is bigger than this."** It's like turning on a light in your heart.

"The Big Idea"

We aren't just "buckets" meant to collect God's blessings; we are meant to be "pipes" that let His goodness flow through us to others.

"Scripture Focus"

"Each of you should give what you have decided in your heart to give, not reluctantly or under compulsion, for God loves a cheerful giver." - 2 Corinthians 9:7

The Two Lakes

In the land where Jesus lived, there are two famous bodies of water. One is the Sea of Galilee. It is full of fish, surrounded by green trees, and teeming with life. Why? Because water flows into it from the mountains and flows out of it *into* a river.

The other is the Dead Sea. Nothing lives there. No fish, no plants, nothing. Why? Because water flows into it, but it has no way to flow out. It just keeps everything for itself until the water becomes salty and stale.

In Christian Living, we want to be like the Sea of Galilee. In theology, we call this **Stewardship**. This is the idea that everything we have, our toys, our money, our time, and even our snacks, doesn't actually "belong" to us. It's all a gift from God, and He lets us manage it. When we share, we keep the water moving, and our lives stay "fresh" and full of life.

The "Cheerful" Secret

Have you ever shared a toy because your mom *made* you do it? You probably handed it over with a frowny face and a heavy sigh. That's called giving "grudgingly."

But God is a **Cheerful Giver**. Think about it: He didn't have to make 1,000 different types of fruit or beautiful sunsets, but He did it because He loves to give! When we share cheerfully, we are acting just like our Father. We realize that we can't ever "run out" of stuff, because God is the one who keeps the supply coming.

More Than Just Money

Sharing isn't just about the coins in your piggy bank. You have three big things you can share:

1. **Your Treasure: Sharing your things or your money with people who have less.**
2. **Your Time: Helping a neighbor pull weeds or playing a game with a lonely sibling.**
3. **Your Talent: Using what you're good at (Week 34) to help someone else for free.**

When we give, we are telling the world, "I trust God to take care of me, so I don't have to hoard everything for myself."

1. Why is it sometimes scary to share something you really like? (Are you afraid you won't get it back or that you'll run out?)

2. How does it feel when someone shares something with you just because they *want* to, not because they *have* to?

3. If you were a "pipe" for God's blessings today, who would you want to "flow" toward first?

This week, try the **"One-Plus" Challenge.** Whenever you get something, maybe a pack of stickers, a bag of treats, or even just some free time, look for a way to share at least "one" part of it with someone else. As you give it away, say in your head: *"God gave this to me, and I'm sharing it for Him."* Watch how much happier you feel being a "Galilee" instead of a "Dead Sea"!

"The Big Idea"

Your life is like a living advertisement for God. When you live with kindness and integrity, you "turn on the light" so others can see the way to Him.

SCRIPTURE FOCUS

"In the same way, let your light shine before others, that they may see your good deeds and glorify your Father in heaven."
- Matthew 5:16

The City on a Hill

Imagine you are lost in a dark forest at night. It's cold, spooky, and you have no idea which way is north. Suddenly, you look up and see a bright city sitting on top of a high hill. The thousands of windows and streetlamps create a glow that can be seen for miles. You don't need a map anymore; you just walk toward the light.

In theology, we call this **The Christian Witness**. Jesus told His followers that they are "the light of the world." He didn't say we *should* be light; He said we are light. Just by being a child of God, you carry a "glow" with you. Your job isn't to create the light (Jesus does that!), but simply to make sure you don't hide it under a "bushel" or a bucket.

Living "Out Loud"

Have you ever seen a movie where the hero says they are the "good guy," but then they act like a villain? It's confusing, right? People watch what we do much more than they listen to what we say.

Shining your light means living in a way that makes people ask, "Why are you like that?"

- When you don't join in when people are making fun of someone.

- When you tell the truth even if it means you might get in trouble.

- When you are happy for a friend who won a prize, even if you wanted to win it yourself.

When you do these "good works," you are like a neon sign pointing up toward God. People see your character and realize that the God you follow must be pretty amazing.

The Reflection Secret

Think about the Moon. The Moon doesn't actually have any light of its own; it's just a big, grey rock. But when it faces the Sun, it reflects the Sun's light so brightly that it can guide travelers at night.

We are like the Moon. If we spend time looking at Jesus, reading His words and talking to Him (Week 41), we automatically start to "glow" with His reflection. You don't have to try really hard to be "shiny." You just have to stay close to the Sun!

1. If your life was a "movie trailer" for God, what would people think He is like based on how you treated people this week?

2. Why do you think people are more likely to believe what we do than what we say?

3. What are some "buckets" (like fear or wanting to be "cool") that sometimes make us want to hide our light?

Find a small candle or a lamp. Turn it on in a dark room and notice how even one tiny light changes the whole space. This week, pick one "Light Action" to do at school or in your neighborhood. It could be standing up for someone, being extra honest, or just being the first one to offer a smile. Remember: you aren't just being a "good kid", you are a "City on a Hill" helping people find their way home!

Part 10:

What Happens Next?

(Eschatology)

We've reached the final leg of our journey! In theology, the study of "last things" or the "end times" is called Eschatology. While some people find this topic scary, for a Christian, it is actually the most exciting part. It's like being at the very end of a long book and finally seeing how the hero wins and everything is made right.

"The Big Idea"

Knowing that Jesus wins in the end changes how we handle our problems today. We live like people who already know the "surprise ending."

"SCRIPTURE FOCUS"

"Since, then, you have been raised with Christ, set your hearts on things above, where Christ is, seated at the right hand of God." - Colossians 3:1

The "Spoilers" of Victory

Imagine you are watching a sports game of your favorite team. Your team is losing, and there are only two minutes left. You feel stressed, upset, and maybe even a little angry. But then, a friend walks in and says, "Don't worry! I recorded this game earlier. Our team makes a huge comeback in the last thirty seconds and wins!"

Suddenly, you aren't stressed anymore. Even when the other team scores again, you just smile. Why? Because you know the **future**. You have a "spoiler" that changes your mood in the present.

Eschatology is God's "spoiler" for us. He tells us that even though the world looks messy right now, Jesus is going to return, fix every broken thing, and reign as King. We don't have to live in fear because we already know who wins.

Eternal Perspective

Most of the time, we focus on what is right in front of us: what's for lunch, what homework is due, or who is being mean to us. Theologians call this "Temporal" (temporary) thinking.

God wants us to have an **Eternal Perspective.**

- **Temporal thinking: "This bad day is the worst thing ever!"**

- **Eternal thinking: "This day is hard, but it's only one tiny dot on a line that goes on forever. God has a perfect world waiting for me."**

When we "seek things which are above," we invest our time in things that last forever, like loving people and knowing God, rather than just trying to get the most toys or the highest score.

The Anchor in the Storm

The Bible calls our hope for the future an "anchor of the soul." An anchor keeps a boat from drifting away when the waves get big. When life gets confusing, our "anchor" is the promise that Jesus is coming back. We live for the future by being faithful today, knowing that our "Commander" is on His way to bring us home.

1. If you knew for sure that you were going to win a huge prize tomorrow, would it be easier to handle a boring chore today? Why?

2. How does knowing that Jesus wins help you stay calm when you see "scary" things in the news or the world?

3. What is one thing you can do today that will still matter 100 years from now?

Take Action

Draw a long, long line on a piece of paper. At the very beginning, draw a tiny dot. That dot represents your life right now. The rest of the line represents eternity with God. This week, whenever you feel frustrated, look at your "timeline" and remember: God's plan for your joy is way bigger than today's problem!

The Big Idea

Heaven isn't just a cloud in the sky; it's a brand-new, physical world where everything sad comes untrue and God lives right among us.

SCRIPTURE FOCUS

"Then J saw "a new heaven and a new earth," for the first heaven and the first earth had passed away, and there was no longer any sea. J saw the Holy City, the new Jerusalem, coming down out of heaven from God, prepared as a bride beautifully dressed for her husband. And J heard a loud voice from the throne saying, "Look! God's dwelling place is now among the people, and he will dwell with them. They will be his people, and God himself will be with them and be their God. 'He will wipe every tear from their eyes. There will be no more death' or mourning or crying or pain, for the old order of things has passed away." - Revelation 21:1-4

When some people think of the future, they imagine sitting on a cold, fluffy cloud, wearing a white robe, and playing a harp forever. To be honest, that sounds a little... boring! But the Bible describes something much more exciting.

In Systematic Theology, we call this the **New Creation**. God isn't going to throw away the world He made; He is going to "heal" it. Imagine your favorite park, but with no trash, no thorns, and no sunburnt grass. Imagine the most beautiful city you've ever seen, but with no crime, no locks on the doors, and everyone is a best friend. That is the "New Jerusalem."

The "No More" List

The coolest thing about this New City is what *isn't* there. Theologians call this the "Via Negativa", defining something by what it lacks. In the New City, there is a "No More" list that makes it the happiest place in existence:

- No more sickness: **No hospitals, no wheelchairs, and no "feeling under the weather."**

- No more sadness: **No more "goodbyes" or lonely nights.**

- No more darkness: **The Bible says God's own glory is so bright we won't even need a sun or a moon!**

- No more sin: **No more "mean voices" in our heads or selfishness in our hearts.**

The Tree of Life returns

Remember way back in **Week 16** when Adam and Eve had to leave the Garden of Eden? They were blocked from the Tree of Life. But in the very last chapter of the Bible, the Tree of Life is back! It's growing right in the middle of the city, and its leaves are for "the healing of the nations."

The story ends right back where it started, but even better. We aren't just in a garden anymore; we are in a magnificent city where everyone has a job to do, things to explore, and a God who walks and talks with them every single day.

Talk It Over

1. If you could design one room in a house in the New City, what would it look like?

2. Why is it important that the New Heaven and New Earth are *physical* places where we can eat, walk, and hug people?

3. Which "No More" on the list are you most excited about?

Take Action

Go outside and find something beautiful, a flower, a cool rock, or a sunset. Now, close your eyes and imagine what that thing would look like if it were "perfected", no decay, no dirt, just pure beauty. This week, whenever you see something broken or sad (like a wilted plant or a rainy day), say to yourself: *"One day, God is going to make that brand new."*

"The Big Idea"

We don't know exactly when Jesus will return, so we live every day like it could be the day, keeping our hearts clean and our hands busy doing His work.

"SCRIPTURE FOCUS"

"Therefore keep watch, because you do not know the day or the hour." - Matthew 25:13

The Surprise Party

Imagine your best friend is coming home from a long trip, and you are throwing them a massive surprise party. You know they are coming home sometime today, but you don't know if it will be at 10:00 AM or 10:00 PM.

What do you do? You don't sit on the porch and stare at the street for twelve hours straight. Instead, you get to work! You blow up the balloons, you bake the cake, and you make sure the house is clean. You keep "one eye on the door" while your hands are busy preparing.

In theology, this is called **Watching and Waiting**. Jesus told several stories (parables) about servants whose master went away. The "good servants" were the ones found doing their jobs faithfully when the master walked through the door.

The Thief in the Night

The Bible uses a strange phrase to describe Jesus' return: He will come "as a thief in the night." This doesn't mean He is coming to steal anything! It means His arrival will be a **total surprise**.

Throughout history, many people have tried to calculate the exact date of the end of the world. They look at blood moons, math equations, and secret codes. But Jesus was very clear: even He (while on earth) didn't claim to know the date—only the Father knows. If someone tells you they've figured out the exact Tuesday Jesus is coming back, you can know for sure they are mistaken!

How to Stay "Ready"

Being "ready" for the King doesn't mean being scared or quitting school to go sit on a mountain. It means living with **Integrity**.

- **Integrity is doing the right thing even when you think no one is looking.**
- It means being the kind of person you would want Jesus to find you being.

If you are being kind to your siblings, talking to your Father in prayer (Week 41), and using your gifts (Week 34), you are already "ready." You don't have to scramble to clean up your life at the last second because you've been living in the light all along.

1. If you knew Jesus was coming back at exactly 4:00 PM today, what is the first thing you would do?

2. Why do you think God keeps the date a secret? How would we act differently if we knew it was 100 years away? What if we knew it was tomorrow?

3. How can we be "excited" about His return instead of "nervous"?

Pick one room or area of your house that is messy. Set a timer for five minutes and see how much you can clean before the "alarm" goes off. As you clean, think: *I want my heart to be ready for Jesus just like I'm making this room ready for a guest.* " This week, practice "living in the ready", try to make every word and action something you'd be happy for the King to see.

"The Big Idea"

The Big Idea: One day, every person will stand before God to give an account of their life. For those who follow Jesus, this is a day of rewards, not of fear.

SCRIPTURE FOCUS

"For we must all appear before the judgment seat of Christ, so that each of us may receive what is due us for the things done while in the body, whether good or bad." - 2 Corinthians 5:10

The Final Award Ceremony

Imagine you are a runner in a long race. You've trained for months, pushed through the cramps, and finally crossed the finish line. After the race, there is a ceremony. The coach calls each runner up to the podium. He doesn't just give out a generic "good job"; he talks about the specific moments where you showed grit, the times you helped a teammate, and the way you didn't give up when it was uphill.

In theology, we call this the **Bema Seat** or the **Judgment Seat of Christ**. For a Christian, this isn't a "courtroom" where we worry about being punished for our sins (remember **Week 26**, Jesus already took that punishment!). Instead, it's more like an award ceremony. It's a moment where God looks at the "movie" of your life and highlights the things you did for Him.

What Is Being Evaluated?

God doesn't look at the things the world thinks are important—like how much money you made or how "famous" you were at school. He looks at the **motive** of your heart.

- **The Secret Actions: The time you shared your lunch when no one was watching.**
- **The Words of Life: The times you used your tongue to encourage instead of tear down.**
- **The Persistence: The times you chose to trust God even when life was really hard (Week 45).**

The Bible says our works will be tested by "fire." Things done for selfish reasons will disappear like wood and hay. But things done out of love for God will remain like gold, silver, and precious stones.

The Ultimate "Well Done"

The greatest reward isn't a gold crown or a trophy. The greatest reward is hearing the Creator of the universe look at you and say, **"Well done, thou good and faithful servant."** Standing before the throne is the moment when all the "hidden" good you did finally comes into the light. It's the moment you realize that every prayer you whispered, every penny you shared, and every time you chose kindness was worth it.

Talk It Over

1. If you were standing before God today, what is one "gold and silver" moment from this past week that you think He would be proud of?

2. Why is it a relief to know that Jesus has already paid for our mistakes, so the judgment is about *rewards* rather than *punishment*?

3. How does knowing that God sees the "secret" good things you do change how you act when you are alone?

Take Action

Find something shiny, like a coin or a piece of foil. Keep it in your pocket today. Every time you touch it, remember that you are "building" with gold and silver every time you choose to love God and others. Try to do one "secret" good deed today that only God will see, knowing that He is already preparing your "Well Done."

"The Big Idea"

The end of the Bible isn't actually an "ending" at all; it's the beginning of the greatest celebration ever, and everyone is invited to the table.

SCRIPTURE FOCUS

"Let us rejoice and be glad and give him glory! For the wedding of the Lamb has come, and his bride has made herself ready." - Revelation 19:7

The Ultimate Victory Party

Think about the best party you have ever been to. Maybe there was unlimited pizza, a massive bounce house, or all your favorite friends laughing together. Now, multiply that feeling by a million.

In the book of Revelation, God gives us a sneak peek of how human history wraps up. It doesn't end with a boring meeting or a quiet fade-out. It ends with a colossal, joyful feast called **The Marriage Supper of the Lamb**. After all the battles are won, all the tears are wiped away, and all the wrongs are made right, God throws a party to celebrate that His family is finally home.

The Bride and the Groom

In theology, the Church (which means all the people who follow Jesus) is often called the "Bride of Christ." That might sound a little funny at first, but think about a wedding day. The groom stands at the front, his face glowing with joy, waiting for his bride to walk down the aisle. He loves her, he chose her, and he promises to take care of her forever.

Jesus is the Groom, and we are the Bride. Throughout history, Jesus has been preparing a place for us, and we have been getting our hearts "ready" for Him. The Marriage Supper is the moment when we are finally reunited with our Savior, never to be separated by sin or death ever again.

Chapter One of the Great Story

You have spent 52 weeks learning about God, the Bible, and Christian living. You've learned about the Trinity, the Fall, Redemption, and the Holy Spirit. But guess what? You haven't reached the end of the story. You've only just finished the introduction!

C.S. Lewis, a famous Christian writer, once said that when we finally reach the New Heaven and New Earth, it will be like turning the page to Chapter One of the Great Story. Everything we do here on earth is just the title page. The real adventure, exploring God's perfect universe and knowing Him more and more every single day, will last forever.

Talk It Over

1. What do you think will be the best part about sitting at a table with Jesus at the Marriage Supper?

2. Looking back over all 52 weeks, what was your favorite "Big Idea" or concept that you learned this year?

3. How does knowing that the story ends with a "party" change how you feel about your future?

Take Action

To celebrate finishing your 52-week theology journey, have a mini "Victory Party" today! Ask your family if you can have your favorite snack or dessert. Before you eat it, say a prayer out loud: *"Thank you, God, for everything I've learned this year. I can't wait for the great feast with You. Help me to keep learning and loving You until that day comes. Amen!"*

www.ingramcontent.com/pod-product-compliance
Lightning Source LLC
Chambersburg PA
CBHW071324140726
47996CB00005B/1808

Table des matières

Kaï

J'ai toujours aimé la maison de mes parents. J'étais le seul parmi mes amis à ne pas être gêné d'être à la maison.

La vie familiale de Michael l'avait ennuyé et agacé, et Damon voulait être là où nous étions. Will avait bien grandi, mais il avait eu besoin d'action. Si les ennuis ne le trouvaient pas, il irait le chercher.

J'avais voulu être à la maison, cependant, et des années plus tard, il était toujours agréable de franchir la porte d'entrée de la maison dans laquelle j'ai grandi.

« Ah ! » Un rugissement lointain retentit alors que j'entrais à l'intérieur.

Je souris en fermant la porte derrière moi, reconnaissant le grognement de Banks. Elle était dans le dojo de mon père, gagnante ou vraiment perdante.

Inspirant, j'aspirai l'odeur pure de l'air frais et des feuilles, toute la maison imprégnée de l'odeur des herbes et des plantes que ma mère cultivait dans le solarium à côté de la cuisine.

J'ai tendu la main, effleurant le philodendron et le bambou en marchant dans le couloir.

Alors que l'extérieur de la maison se mélangeait avec le style de campagne anglais des autres maisons du quartier, l'intérieur était très différent. Le design épuré, épuré et minimaliste correspondait au goût de mon père. Les éléments naturels comme les plantes, les pierres et la lumière du soleil ont fait entrer l'extérieur, ce qui a aidé pendant les longs mois d'hiver à l'intérieur.

Mais alors que le style japonais privilégiait le blanc et le brillant, l'influence de ma mère était également évidente. Des sols en teck foncé, des tapis et des couleurs éclaboussé ici et là. C'était toujours comme si vous marchiez dans une grotte confortable. Mes parents étaient doués pour les compromis et je me suis toujours sentie en sécurité ici.

Des bougies brillaient à l'intérieur de leurs appliques murales, prêtes pour la Nuit du Feu. Noël n'était pas avant quelques jours, et même si mes parents ne se sont pas vraiment précipités pour se livrer à la nouvelle tradition de Noël à Thunder Bay, ils savaient que Jett et Mads adoraient ça, alors ils ont accepté.

Je levai les mains, soufflant de l'air chaud contre mes doigts glacés, sentant mon alliance glacée.

"Grand-mère..." J'ai entendu Jett rire.

Jetant un coup d'œil au coin de la rue, je m'appuyai contre le cadre de la porte et regardai ma mère se détourner et rire alors que ma fille lui lançait une pincée de farine, son nez et ses joues également saupoudrés de poudre.

J'ai baissé les yeux en voyant les pieds nus de ma fille qui dépassaient derrière elle alors qu'elle s'agenouillait sur un tabouret et continuait à pétrir la pâte. Il y a huit ans, je pouvais mettre ces choses dans ma bouche. Elle grandissait trop vite, et je voulais en quelque sorte que le temps s'arrête.

Ou je voulais plus d'enfants.

C'était jusqu'à ce que j'aille chez Damon et que je me précipite par la porte d'entrée dix minutes plus tard avec une migraine. Leur journée de nounou était bien, et je n'allais même pas prétendre que je ne comprenais pas pourquoi.

J'ai regardé ma mère et ma fille travailler côte à côte, heureuse qu'elles soient heureuses. Mads était venu avec sa mère et sa sœur, mais il était introuvable pour le moment. Probablement caché dans la cave à vin, en train de lire. Il avait un coin où se cacher dans chaque maison. Un coin au fond du labyrinthe du jardin à la maison. Un placard chez Damon. La galerie de St. Killian's. Un siège près de la fenêtre derrière les rideaux chez Will.

Alors que je m'inquiétais pour lui d'une manière que je ne m'inquiétais pas pour Jett, j'ai toujours su où le trouver. Il ne m'a jamais fait peur.

"Je dois aller aux toilettes", a annoncé Jett en sautant du tabouret.

"Lavez-vous les mains", lui a dit ma mère.

Jett se précipita vers la salle de boue, essuya ses mains enduites de farine sur son petit tablier, et ferma la porte.

Je suis entré dans la cuisine. "Tu es une bonne maman, tu sais ?"
Ma mère m'a jeté un coup d'œil, s'arrêtant avec ses mains dans le bol.
"Tu aurais dû avoir une maison pleine d'enfants", lui ai-je dit.

Elle sourit pour elle-même, travaillant la pâte alors que je venais derrière elle et enroulais mes bras autour de ses épaules. J'ai glissé mon menton dans son cou avec espièglerie.

« Tu étais assez », dit-elle.

« Peut-être trop ?

"Oh ouais." Elle s'est moquée. "Beaucoup trop."

Je ris, appréciant la plaisanterie même si elle ne mentait pas vraiment. Se faire arrêter et emprisonner était un enfer pour eux, et j'avais assez honte de la déception et du chagrin que j'avais causés, mais encore plus depuis que j'étais leur seul enfant. Je me détestais de ne pas faire mieux.

Je baissai les yeux sur le petit pendentif en argent caché derrière le tablier de ma mère. Sainte Félicité de Rome. Je la serrai plus fort et elle s'arrêta, me laissant faire.

Elle adorait être grand-mère.

« Ils sont toujours au dojo ? demandai-je en me reculant et en prenant une des tranches de mandarine du petit bol qui était probablement le goûter de Jett.

Je l'ai mis dans ma bouche.

"Depuis deux heures maintenant," répondit ma mère. "Allez voir si elle est encore en vie."

"Ma femme peut prendre ce vieil homme."

Je me dirigeai vers le couloir, sentant les yeux de ma mère sur moi. Je m'arrêtai et jetai un regard par-dessus mon épaule en secouant la tête. "Peu importe. Je savais que c'était stupide quand je l'ai dit.

Elle rit, nous savions tous les deux que nous n'avions toujours pas vu une seule personne qui pourrait prendre mon père.

« Tu viens ce soir, n'est-ce pas ? » Je lui ai demandé.

Je vis sa poitrine tomber dans un profond soupir et ses yeux voilés me lançaient un regard. "J'ai envie d'une soirée calme, merci."

"Que veux-tu dire? Ce sera calme.

Elle haussa les sourcils et je réprimai mon rire.

OK OK.

« Peut-être », dit-elle en retournant à son travail.

Je secouai la tête et me tournai en souriant. Il vaudrait mieux que ce soit putain de calme ce soir.

9

Je descendis le couloir, sortis par la porte coulissante et pénétrai dans le jardin de rocaille. Les arbres miniatures, les buissons et les étangs recouverts de neige ont créé une oasis de paix en plein air au centre de la maison. Banks et moi avions créé quelque chose comme ça chez nous à Meridian City, ce qui était un exploit, étant donné qu'elle préférait la prolifération sauvage et le labyrinthe de jardin de notre maison ici. J'ai privilégié le paysage plus stylisé avec lequel j'ai grandi.

Les nuages étaient bas, promettant plus de neige ce soir, et je pouvais sentir la glace dans l'air. Devil's Night était dans notre sang, mais Fire Night commençait à devenir mon préféré. J'ai adoré cette période de l'année.

En arrivant à la porte, j'ouvris le panneau et les remarquai immédiatement, s'entraînant au centre du dojo alors que je me glissais tranquillement à l'intérieur et fermais le fusuma derrière moi.

Les festivités en ville avaient déjà commencé et nous allions être en retard, mais mon cœur se gonflait et je ne pouvais pas encore l'interrompre. J'adorais regarder Banks et mon père. J'adorais la voir passer du temps avec mes parents.

« Tu me regardes », a dit mon père en bloquant son coup de pied.

Elle l'a chargé, les cheveux qui s'étaient détachés de sa queue de cheval pendant dans ses yeux, et la sueur couvrant la poitrine et le cou de mon père.

Il a bloqué un coup de poing, avançant sur elle. « Arrête de me regarder », aboya-t-il. Elle s'est retirée alors qu'elle aurait dû le contourner pour gagner du temps.

« Quand tu me regardes, tu ne vois pas », lui dit-il. "Il faut tout voir."

Elle grogna, lançant un coup de poing puis un coup de pied haut, ce dernier qu'il attrapa et rejeta sans même un froncement de sourcils noirs et sévères. Mads lui ressemblait de plus en plus chaque jour.

Je croisai les bras sur ma poitrine, restant dans l'ombre de la poutre qui s'étendait jusqu'au plafond tandis que je regardais ma femme trébucher sur le côté, respirant difficilement et déjà épuisée.

Nous nous entraînions à Sensou plusieurs fois par semaine. Elle était en pleine forme. Ou aurait dû l'être.

Mon père s'est approché d'elle, vêtu d'un pantalon noir ample avec plus de sueur matant les cheveux poivre et sel sur son front.

Il la releva et la fixa. "Ferme tes yeux."

Elle me tournait le dos, mais elle n'avait pas dû écouter, car il l'a répété.

"Fermez les yeux", a-t-il exhorté.

Elle se tenait là, et après un moment, j'ai remarqué ses épaules carrées et sa respiration régulière.

"In", dit-il, inspirant avec elle. "Dehors."

Un sourire s'étira sur mes lèvres alors que quelques flocons de neige flottaient sur le sol immobile devant les fenêtres.

Je me suis souvenu de cette leçon.

"Encore," dit-il.

Ils inspirèrent et expirèrent lentement tandis qu'il attendait que l'esprit de Banks s'éclaircisse.

« Gardez les yeux fermés », ordonna-t-il.

Ses bras pendaient à ses côtés et elle continuait sa respiration régulière.

"Est-ce que tu me vois?" Il a demandé. "Avez-vous toujours l'image de moi devant vous dans votre tête?"

"Oui," j'ai entendu sa réponse. "Que vois-tu?" Elle hésita.

« Que voyez-vous exactement ? » il a précisé.

12

"Tes yeux."

"Et?"

"Ton visage."

Il l'étudia un moment puis continua. "Dézoomer. Maintenant que vois tu?"

« La… la pièce autour de vous ? » elle a répondu.

Il s'avança, calmant sa voix. « Respire », murmura-t-il. "Que voyez-vous d'autre? Fais-moi bouger.

Elle pencha un peu la tête, comme si elle regardait une scène dans sa tête.

"Vos bras et vos jambes."

"Et?"

« Tes pieds », dit-elle. "Ils changent."

Finalement, il hocha la tête comme si elle avait enfin vu ce qu'il voulait qu'elle voie. « Si vous regardez de trop près, vous ne verrez rien. Comprenez vous?" Elle acquiesça.

Elle avait besoin de voir mais pas spécifiquement, comme si tout dans sa vision, même la périphérie, était au centre de ses préoccupations. Je les ai vus, mais j'ai aussi vu Frost, le chat de ma mère respirant tranquillement sur le chevron au-dessus. Je pouvais voir Banks et mon père face à face, mais aussi les flocons de neige flottant presque dans l'air à l'extérieur.

13

"Ouvrez les yeux", ordonna-t-il.

Il fit un pas en arrière et se mit en position de combat. "Dézoomer."

Avant qu'elle ne puisse se mettre en position, il fit un pas et lança un poing. Elle leva la main et la repoussa, puis esquiva rapidement un autre poing lorsqu'il rentra.

J'ai souris.

Et puis, ils y étaient. Elle a sauté dans une position, et en moins d'un instant, les poings et les pieds ont volé partout. Les bras et les jambes se balayèrent, volant, et des grognements remplirent la pièce alors qu'il attrapait sa cuisse et qu'elle posait un poing sur son côté.

Ils se déplaçaient, Banks avançant vers lui puis lui vers elle, leurs pas voletant sur le tapis alors qu'ils tournaient l'un autour de l'autre. Une main écarta un poing avant que l'autre n'entre et en repousse un autre.

Je ne pouvais même pas suivre ce que chacun d'eux faisait, ils se déplaçaient si vite. Bras levé, poignet frappant le poignet, puis les coups de pied volant dans les airs pour être défendus.

C'était comme une danse.

Mon cœur battait la chamade alors que je regardais un sourire traverser le visage de mon père, ma respiration s'arrêtant un instant, puis...

Il recula de quelques pas, elle entra avec un autre coup de poing, et il attrapa ses poignets juste à temps, l'arrêtant.

Il a souri, Banks figée, alors que des respirations difficiles remplissaient la pièce et qu'elle fixait mon père.

Jésus. Il s'était arrêté le premier. Elle l'avait épuisé.

Je couvris mon sourire de ma main, la fierté gonflant mon cœur. Bientôt, Mads et Jett seraient comme ça, et même si je n'avais jamais prévu de danger dans notre avenir, je savais que c'était possible. Je respirais plus facilement, sachant que ma famille était au moins un peu préparée à tout ce qui pourrait arriver.

Mais pas ce soir. Ce soir, c'était pour faire la fête.

La relâchant, il se redressa et s'avança vers elle, prenant ses épaules. Ils n'avaient pas reconnu ma présence, mais mon père savait probablement que j'étais là.

Son corps bougeait de haut en bas alors qu'elle tentait de reprendre son souffle.

Il baissa les yeux. "Bien," dit-il d'une voix douce.

15

Elle le regarda, mais je vis alors sa tête tomber et sa mâchoire se contracter.

« Maintenant, va t'amuser ce soir », lui dit-il.

Je me suis écarté du mur et j'ai marché vers Banks quand elle s'est retournée et a rencontré mon regard. Des larmes coulaient dans les siennes, et elle détourna rapidement les yeux alors que mon père se dirigeait vers moi, hochant la tête en passant devant moi.

Inclinant son menton vers le haut, j'ai regardé son beau visage, brillant d'une légère couche de sueur et ses yeux verts brillants.

Elle jeta un coup d'œil à mon père, Jett le croisant dans la rocaille et saluant son grand-père au passage. Il retourna le geste.

« Tu as beaucoup de chance, tu sais ? dit Banks, la voix tremblante. "Il est fier de toi."

J'ai touché son visage.

« Tu as tellement de chance », a-t-elle répété, et j'ai pu entendre le craquement dans sa voix.

La faisant entrer, je l'embrassai sur le front alors qu'elle tremblait de plus en plus de larmes.

"Il est fier de toi aussi," murmurai-je.

La prenant dans mes bras, je la serrai fort, détestant tous les souvenirs qu'elle n'avait

16

pas. Comment elle avait souffert sans parents, et combien j'avais pris pour acquis. Mon père n'a jamais été particulièrement chaleureux, mais il était loin d'Evans Crist ou de Gabriel putain de Torrance. C'était un homme bon et elle avait plus de trente ans avant de savoir ce que ressentait un vrai père.

"Il est si fier de toi, bébé," lui ai-je répété.

Chaud ou pas, mon père n'a jamais été là pour aucun d'entre nous. Nous avons tous eu de la chance.

Jett s'est approchée, ses bras s'enroulant autour de nous – aussi loin qu'elle pouvait en tout cas – et s'est jointe à l'étreinte. Je ris en tenant mes filles.

Au bout d'un moment, Banks s'essuya les yeux et inspira profondément, reculant un peu.

Elle baissa les yeux sur notre fille. « M'aider à me maquiller ? » elle a demandé.

Mais je les ai arrêtés juste là, disant à Jett à la place: "En fait, va demander à grand-mère comment rempoter une châtaigne", ai-je dit. "Je dois d'abord aider maman avec sa douche."

"Kai..." réprimanda Banks.

*Quoi?*Je restai bouche bée. A quoi servaient les grands-parents de toute façon ?

....

"Tu n'as pas froid ?" Banks a glissé ses bras autour des miens, m'étreignant pour me réchauffer.

J'ai inhalé l'air vif du soir et soufflé la vapeur, absorbant la neige accrochée aux conifères et les branches nues et noires des érables s'étendant dans le ciel nocturne.

"J'adore ça", lui ai-je dit, en écoutant alors que nous nous tenions devant la maison de mes parents une heure plus tard. "Tout est si calme."

Je la regardai, admirant qu'il lui ait à peine fallu du temps pour s'habiller. Sa robe bustier rouge scintillait, magnifique avec ses cheveux noirs bouclés et épinglés sur le côté au niveau de la nuque. Elle était magnifique.

Elle et Jett avaient tous deux décoré leurs visages, ressemblant à de mignons clowns avec des formes de diamants blancs sur les yeux et des bijoux collés aux pointes.

18

J'ai jeté la cape noire autour d'elle et je l'ai attachée alors qu'elle fouillait dans la poche intérieure et enfilait ses gants.

« Le froid ralentit la propagation des molécules », expliquai-je. "Moins de pollution. L'air est si pur.

Et tranquille. J'ai le plus aimé l'hiver pour cette raison. Les étoiles perçaient à travers les nuages et vous pouviez entendre de l'eau au loin, bien qu'il n'y ait pas d'eau à proximité. La couverture gelée sur la terre dans la nuit noire a tellement fait taire le monde que vous pouviez entendre des choses que vous ne pouviez pas normalement entendre.

C'était obsédant.

« La neige arrive », m'a-t-elle dit. "Nous ferions mieux de nous dépêcher."

Ouais. "Je profite juste du calme avant la tempête", ai-je taquiné.

Et je ne parlais pas de la neige. Ma mère avait raison. Le drame se produisait toujours lorsque la famille se réunissait.

Mads est sorti de la maison, ajustant sa cravate noire sur sa chemise et son costume noirs, et Jett est passé en courant devant lui et s'est approché de moi.

Je l'ai prise dans mes bras, sa robe rose et ses collants blancs choisis par sa mère qui n'a jamais porté de rose de sa vie. Déjà.

Elle me sourit, ses dents blanches me regardant à travers ses lèvres rouges. "Fire Night est mon préféré", a déclaré Jett, regardant les lanternes scintillantes qui bordent l'allée.

« Tu es prêt à allumer d'autres bougies ? » J'ai demandé.

Elle acquiesça. « Pouvons-nous marcher ? »

J'ouvris la bouche pour lui dire non, sachant que ce n'était pas une escapade rapide, surtout avec Banks dans une robe longue et des talons hauts, mais...

Sa mère a resserré sa cape autour d'elle et a gazouillé: "Absolument."

J'ai posé Jett et pris sa main, elle et Mads marchant entre Banks et moi alors que nous partions.

La maison de mes parents était de l'autre côté de la ville par rapport à St. Killian's, et même si la randonnée devait être froide, je ne me plaindrais pas de pouvoir profiter de la soirée un peu plus longtemps. J'espérais juste que Banks ne s'était pas foulé la cheville en chemin.

La lune brillait au-dessus de nos têtes alors que nous traversions la rue et nous promenions dans le parc, d'autres lanternes traçant notre chemin avec leur lumière de feu.

C'était la règle ce soir. Pas de lumières électriques.

Non pas que ce soit une loi ou quoi que ce soit que nous imposions, mais tout avait l'air différent à la lueur du feu, et je ne savais pas lequel d'entre nous établissait la norme, mais tout le monde semblait d'accord pour dire que c'était magnifique.

En un rien de temps, c'était la tradition. Une fois le soleil couché au solstice d'hiver,
Thunder Bay était presque entièrement éclairée par le feu – bougies, lanternes, feux de joie…

Des voix portées par la brise, le chœur de la cathédrale chantant au loin et réchauffant le givre dans l'air et les racines endormies sous nos pieds.

Regardant à gauche, j'ai vu les incendies dans le village, une grande partie de la ville appréciant les festivités et le défilé, et lentement, j'ai tourné la tête, voyant toutes les flammes vacillantes parsemant la ville.

21

Rien, pas même Devil's Night, n'était plus magique, car ce soir était la nuit la plus longue de l'année. C'était spécial.

La neige a commencé à tomber autour de nous plus lourdement, et Mads et Jett ont ouvert la voie sur le pont, des flocons parsemant leurs cheveux noirs.

"Voir!" Jett pointa par-dessus le bord, vers la rivière qui coulait en contrebas.

Un petit remorqueur s'est dirigé vers nous, des lumières blanches décorant son extérieur, et nous sommes tous restés là pendant que les enfants le regardaient disparaître sous le pont, puis ils se sont précipités de l'autre côté pour le voir sortir.

Banks et moi restâmes à contempler le village, au-delà duquel se trouvaient Cold Point, Deadlow Island et notre hôtel, Coldfire Inn. La musique, les lumières, la ville habillée de neige… J'ai inhalé longuement et profondément, resserrant mes bras autour d'elle et me contentant de rester à cet endroit toute la nuit.

« J'aime notre vie », murmura-t-elle en regardant la rivière.

Appuyant mes lèvres sur sa tempe, je fermai les yeux, le sentant aussi.

Satisfaction absolue pendant ces rares moments de calme.

Mais je soupirai, sachant qu'il faudrait trois secondes à son frère pour tout foutre en l'air ce soir.

Michael et Will pourraient prendre un peu plus de temps.

Nous sommes partis, traversant le pont et traversant la ruelle tranquille jusqu'à St. Killian, des bols de feu dansant le long de la longue allée et des torches postées sur la maison autour du périmètre.

Les yeux de Jett s'illuminèrent d'excitation.

Rika l'a fait pour les enfants, mais l'idée derrière Fire Night était celle de Winter.

"Voilà les garçons !" Jett a crié, la neige tombant un peu plus lourde.

J'ai hoché la tête, voyant les enfants de Damon courir sous la canopée des arbres sur le côté, jouant à cache-cache dans le noir.

« Va jouer », lui ai-je dit.

Elle s'est enfuie, se cachant derrière une malle, ses Mary Janes noires brillantes soulevant la neige alors que la vapeur s'échappait de sa bouche, révélant sa position.

23

Mads monta les marches et vira immédiatement dans les escaliers, sa cachette préférée sur la gauche.

Banks se pressa contre moi, touchant ses lèvres aux miennes et les tenant pendant plusieurs secondes. "Je dois parler à Em et Rika, d'accord?" J'ai hoché la tête, la laissant partir.

Elle monta l'escalier en colimaçon, la balustrade habillée de conifères et de rubans, et je levai les yeux vers elle, la regardant disparaître dans la galerie sombre au-dessus. Ensuite, je tendis la main et cassai le bouton d'une rose du bouquet sur la petite table et l'installai dans mon revers.

Aucun invité n'était encore arrivé, les candélabres toujours éteints et l'arbre éteint. Les enfants ont ri et crié à l'extérieur alors que la neige tombait du ciel, et je me suis dirigé vers la fenêtre pour les regarder jouer avant que tous les événements de la nuit ne commencent.

Mais ensuite, j'ai entendu quelque chose au-dessus de moi et j'ai levé les yeux, les yeux écarquillés lorsque j'ai repéré Octavia suspendue à la balustrade donnant sur le deuxième étage au-dessus.

« Tavi ! » J'ai éclaté.

L'épée d'une main, elle pendait de l'autre, son petit visage gravé de colère.

Mais ensuite, elle a glissé et est tombée, et j'ai haleté, tirant et l'attrapant dans mes bras. "Oh merde. Que diable?"

Je la berçai, mon cœur dans ma putain de gorge alors que je resserrais ma prise autour de son petit corps, mes ongles s'enfonçant dans son manteau de pirate noir brodé et ses bottes en cuir.

Je baissai les yeux, rencontrant son air renfrogné. « Ça va ? »

"Je vais te trancher la gorge, espèce de chien !" Et elle a enfoncé la lame en plastique de son épée-jouet dans mon cou.

Oh, Jésus. J'ai roulé des yeux.

Je l'ai soulevée et l'ai jetée par-dessus mon épaule, marchant vers la cuisine.

"Et tu es définitivement la fille de ton père," la taquinai-je.

Aucune idée de ce qui aurait pu lui arriver. Et zéro soin.

"Lâchez-moi !"

« Pas une chance », ai-je rétorqué. « À quoi pensais-tu, hein ? »

"Je me faufilais sur la vermine!" expliqua-t-elle, essayant de se tortiller et de sortir de ma prise. "Il essaie de me débaucher l'équipage !"

J'entrai dans la cuisine, évitant les traiteurs, et posai Octavia sur un comptoir latéral, à l'écart.

"Tu dois être prudent." Je baissais les yeux vers ses yeux noirs. "Comprenez vous?"

Elle a creusé ses sourcils, accentuant la petite cicatrice qu'elle avait sur l'œil droit suite à une chute qu'elle avait subie quand elle avait deux ans.

"Tes parents ne seraient pas contents si tu ouvrais ton petit crâne." Je me dirigeai vers le réfrigérateur et en sortis une boîte de jus, y glissant la paille pour elle. « Ton père ne pourrait pas le supporter. Tu sais à quel point tout le monde t'aime ?

"Je n'ai peur de rien."

Je m'arrêtai et la regardai. Ce genre de discours pouvait mener sur un chemin sombre que je connaissais bien.

Je me suis approché et au lieu de lui donner le jus, je l'ai posé sur le comptoir et j'ai planté mes paumes de chaque côté d'elle. « Regarde-moi », lui ai-je dit. « Je sais que tu n'as pas peur. Mais la peur et la prudence sont deux choses différentes. S'il vous arrivait quelque chose, votre père n'y survivrait pas. Comprends-tu cela?"

À peine âgée de cinq ans, elle me fixait d'un air vide.

"Un vrai capitaine donne l'exemple." J'ai tapoté sa tête avec mon doigt. « Un vrai capitaine utilise sa tête, d'accord ? Un jour, vous allez apprendre que votre vie peut changer en un instant. La prudence est intelligente, et les gens intelligents trouvent un meilleur moyen.

"Mais comment apprenez-vous la différence entre la peur et la prudence?" demanda une voix.

Je me redressai et me retournai, voyant Damon s'attarder dans l'embrasure de la porte. Il était partiellement habillé pour ce soir – pantalon noir et chaussures cirées, les cheveux en place. Mais il lui manquait toujours sa veste et sa cravate, et sa chemise blanche avait les manches retroussées.

« Par expérience », a-t-il répondu quand je ne l'ai pas fait.

Il s'est approché et ma colonne vertébrale s'est durcie, parce que nos styles parentaux étaient devenus juste un autre domaine dans lequel nous étions fortement en désaccord. Avec quelqu'un en dehors de

27

notre famille, je m'en ficherais, mais quand mes enfants étaient habitués à plus de discipline, il devenait de plus en plus difficile d'expliquer pourquoi les siens étaient autorisés à se balancer des chevrons.

"Et grâce aux conseils de personnes qui en savent plus", ai-je répliqué alors qu'il prenait sa fille dans ses bras.

Il regarda Octavia en haussant un sourcil. "Les gens qui se sont soumis aux règles et ont perdu leur imagination, il veut dire."

J'ai masqué mes yeux. "Est-ce que papa te laisse traverser les rues tout seul?" Je lui ai demandé.

Elle a sucé son jus, sachant même à ce jeune âge ne pas s'impliquer dans nos querelles stupides.

« Parce que, comme je l'ai dit... » Je souris amèrement à Damon. "" Des conseils de personnes qui en savent plus. ""

"Et comment déterminez-vous ceux qui valent la peine d'être écoutés?" demanda-t-il à Octavia, mais il essayait juste de me faire chier. « Non. Tu t'écoutes. »

« Et pendant que vous faites cela, lui ai-je dit, n'oubliez pas de vous rappeler que les choix ont des conséquences avec lesquelles vous devrez vivre pour le reste de votre vie.

Vous ferez de meilleurs choix avec des conseils.

"As tu?" Damon m'a finalement regardé, notre séjour en prison n'ayant pas besoin d'un rappel pour que je comprenne ce qu'il voulait dire.

Piquer.

Il venait d'un mauvais foyer. Je viens d'un bon. Nous sommes tous les deux allés en prison.

Dieu, je le détestais.

Je veux dire, je sauterais certainement d'un pont pour lui, mais...

Il a pris sa fille et son sourire satisfait de lui-même et est sorti, et j'ai combattu l'envie de lui lancer quelque chose à l'arrière de la tête.

Je viens de sauver la vie de son enfant.

Ou, au moins quelques os cassés.

Mais bon... ça aurait été une expérience pour elle. Mettez des poils sur sa poitrine. Rawr.

Je sortis à grands pas de la cuisine, l'odeur sucrée de vanille des biscuits, macarons et autres friandises remplissant la maison tandis que les serveurs transportaient les plateaux jusqu'à la salle à manger.

29

Madden avait rejoint Ivar pour allumer les candélabres, chacun faisant sa ronde autour de la maison, et je me dirigeai vers la salle de bal mais m'arrêtai, revoyant Damon.

Les lumières s'étaient éteintes, les bougies brillaient sur le sol doré et rouge alors que des guirlandes de vacances de conifères, de gui et de prunes à sucre drapaient le manteau à droite, assorties à celles enroulées autour de la rampe de l'escalier derrière moi.

La piste de danse était encore presque vide, à l'exception de ma femme qui dansait avec son frère.

Me reculant, je croisai les bras sur ma poitrine, m'adoucissant à leur vue ensemble. OK OK. Je ne le détestais pas. Je ne pouvais pas haïr quelqu'un qui l'aimait.

Il la pencha en arrière et tourna avec elle, et elle sourit si largement avant de rire et de jeter ses bras autour de lui alors qu'il allait de plus en plus vite.

Je souris en les regardant.

À proximité, Rika a dansé avec Jett, tous deux regardant leurs pieds pendant que Rika comptait, aidant Jett à faire les pas. Sa robe noire étirée avec la petite bosse de bébé, maintenant environ cinq mois.

Les filles de Will, Indie et Finn, tournoyaient autour des couples, prétendant qu'ils étaient des danseurs de ballet, les plumes noires dans les cheveux de Finn me faisant un peu mal au ventre à ce souvenir. On aurait dit qu'hier, Banks et moi étions dans la salle de bal du pape, regardant la mère de Damon, vêtue de ses plumes noires, se déplacer sur le sol comme un fantôme. Un frisson parcourut ma colonne vertébrale.

« Kai ? » quelqu'un a dit.

J'ai regardé derrière moi et j'ai vu Winter descendre les escaliers en tenant la balustrade à deux mains.

J'ai tendu la main vers elle, la guidant vers moi. "Ouais, ici," dis-je. "Tu m'as senti ?"

Sinon, comment aurait-elle su que c'était moi ?

Elle éclata de rire en me rejoignant à mes côtés. "Mm-hmm. Tu sens bon.

Je souris, tournant les yeux vers la salle de bal. Mon fils avait disparu, et Ivarsen avait rejoint ses frères, nous dépassant en courant vers la salle à manger et les confiseries, sans doute.

Les phares se sont approchés à l'extérieur, les invités ont commencé à arriver.

31

"Octavia ne veut pas aller au cachot ce soir", m'a dit Winter.

"Alors Mads n'ira pas non plus."

"Non."

C'est pourquoi elle me l'a dit, alors j'étais prêt. Pendant que les adultes dansaient toute la nuit ou participaient aux réjouissances des festivités, les enfants allaient vivre leur propre aventure au théâtre. Jusqu'à minuit, en tout cas, quand ils pourraient rentrer à la maison et ouvrir les cadeaux.

L'hiver avait fait du beau travail, rendant cette période de l'année spéciale. Elle adorait Noël mais avait toujours l'impression que la journée était douce-amère, car cela signifiait que la saison était pratiquement terminée. Nous avons commencé nos festivités au solstice maintenant, heureux de profiter que nous avions encore des jours de joie devant nous.

"C'est une enfant très chanceuse", a déclaré Winter. "Beaucoup de gens qui raffolent d'elle."

J'ai hoché la tête, voyant une ombre au deuxième étage. Mads s'était de nouveau retiré dans sa cachette.

« C'est une aventurière », ai-je répondu. « Mads ne l'est pas. Il peut vivre par procuration à travers elle.

"Et elle aime pouvoir le traîner n'importe où", a-t-elle ajouté, "et il ne se fâche jamais avec elle. Ses frères ne sont... pas si flexibles.

Ses frères avaient des problèmes. Au moins, Mads a donné le bon exemple.

Les haut-parleurs s'éteignirent alors que l'orchestre finissait de s'accorder, le silence remplissant l'air dans toute la maison.

"J'adore ce son," murmura Winter.

« Quel son ? »

"Le courant d'air de cet ancien endroit qui s'abat sur les flammes", a-t-elle déclaré. "Tu l'entends ?"

J'ai formé mes oreilles, le vent hurlant à travers les étages au-dessus de nous, leurs rafales faisant vaciller les flammes.

Les cheveux sur ma nuque se sont dressés.

"On dirait des fantômes", murmura-t-elle. "Tout est plus beau à la lueur du feu, n'est-ce pas ?"

Je la regardai, ses longs cils tombant sur des yeux qui ne pouvaient plus rien voir de beau, mais cela ne signifiait pas non plus que

33

rien n'était perdu pour elle. Elle le voyait juste différemment maintenant.

Me retournant, je pris sa main dans la mienne et sa taille dans l'autre, et la guidai sur la piste de danse. "Tenir."

Ses lèvres s'étirèrent en un grand sourire, et nous glissâmes, moi la conduisant sans musique alors que des mèches de cheveux tombaient sur son visage. Sa robe noire se déployait derrière elle et les rubans rouges dans ses cheveux flottaient.

« Tu es plutôt doué », m'a-t-elle dit.

"Sous le choc?"

"Eh bien..." Elle haussa les épaules, sans donner plus de détails.

Nous tournâmes et bougeâmes, de plus en plus vite jusqu'à ce qu'elle glousse, mais elle ne perdit jamais pied, plus légère que l'air dans mes bras.

Je suppose qu'elle pensait que je n'excellais qu'au combat, mais ma mère aussi a élevé un gentleman.

« Ne donnez jamais une épée à un homme qui ne sait pas danser », récitai-je Confucius tandis que nous ralentissions.

Elle fronça les sourcils, respirant difficilement. "Pourquoi?"

"Parce qu'une arme de mort ne devrait pas être entre les mains de quelqu'un qui n'a pas vécu."

Vous ne pouvez pas parler pour un monde quand vous ne comprenez qu'un seul point de vue.

Je m'arrêtai et la fixai, une idée se formant. "Je veux que tu apprennes à danser à Mads et Jett."

Elle pencha la tête.

Pourquoi n'y avais-je pas pensé il y a des années ? Je supposais qu'avoir une bonne éducation et apprendre à se défendre les rendrait forts, mais j'avais encore le temps d'encourager ce qui les rendait heureux. Mads détesterait danser, mais un jour, il pourrait apprécier la connaissance.

Après un moment, elle hocha la tête. "D'accord."

Juste à ce moment, Damon intervint, prenant la main et la taille de sa femme dans les siennes. "Pardon."

J'ai reculé, le laissant entrer, et j'étais sur le point d'aller attraper ma propre femme quand je l'ai déjà vue se diriger vers moi.

"Les invités arrivent", a-t-elle dit. « Allons allumer le lustre. Oh c'est vrai.

35

« Jett », ai-je appelé en agitant ma fille vers moi. « Indé ? Finlandais?"

Les invités ont commencé à arriver à la dérive, Rika et Michael se tenant près de la porte pour saluer les gens pendant que les contrôleurs de manteaux prenaient les châles et les gants des dames. Emory, vêtue de vert et ses cheveux tirés en une queue de cheval basse et des boucles tombant dans son dos, encercla le lustre, distribuant des marqueurs et des feuilles de basilic à tous les enfants.

Répartis sur le sol du hall, les invités se sont déplacés autour d'eux pour regarder les enfants écrire leurs souhaits pour la nouvelle année à venir sur les feuilles au marqueur argenté, puis se sont levés, les allumant avec une bougie du lustre.

« Pourquoi le brûle-t-on ? » demanda Gunnar alors que Dag laissait tomber sa feuille de cendre dans le bol en cuivre qu'Emmy tenait.

"Cela libère le souhait dans l'univers", a expliqué Indie.

"Eh bien, j'ai souhaité la gloire l'année dernière", a rétorqué sa sœur, "et cela ne s'est pas réalisé. Je pense que nous faisons cela mal.

J'ai souri en regardant tous les enfants, un par un, se lever et jeter leurs feuilles brûlantes dans le plat.

"Ce n'est pas encore devenu réalité", a ajouté Winter.

Will a commencé le rituel il y a environ huit ans. Une nouvelle tradition. Une façon de garder la cérémonie dans nos vies et quelque chose d'amusant dont les enfants se souviendront et qu'ils transmettront peut-être un jour à leurs propres enfants.

Mon regard s'est arrêté sur Mads, le voyant tenir sa feuille devant la flamme, mais au lieu de l'allumer, il l'a retirée. Le glissant dans sa veste de costume, il se tourna pour aider Octavia, stabilisant sa main alors qu'elle touchait la feuille à la flamme.

Une silhouette est apparue dans l'escalier, et j'ai levé les yeux, voyant Athos descendre dans une robe argentée extrêmement moulante avec un décolleté en V décolleté que j'aurais du mal à voir ma fille porter quand elle avait dix-sept ans.

Son visage brillait de maquillage gris et blanc autour de ses yeux, et ses cheveux pendaient dans son dos avec une paire de petits bois fixés sur sa tête, la faisant ressembler à quelque chose du Songe d'une nuit d'été.

Alex lui avait appris à se maquiller quand elle avait dix ans, mais malheureusement, Alex n'était pas là pour subir la colère de Michael ce soir. Elle et Aydin passaient les vacances avec sa famille à New York, et il nous manquait aussi Micah et Rory, qui étaient aux Fidji.

Misha et Ryen étaient invités, mais je doutais qu'ils se montrent.

Michael s'approcha, se tournant pour garder ses yeux sur elle alors qu'elle passait.

"Vous portez ça au lock-in?"

"Au bal."

"Nous avons eu cette conversation," expliqua-t-il alors qu'elle continuait à marcher. « Vingt et un ans et plus, Athos.

"Heureusement, mon père est propriétaire de l'endroit", a-t-elle lancé en arrière.

Je reniflai en la regardant disparaître dans la salle de bal.

Michael se frotta le visage avec sa main. "Je ne sais même pas pourquoi j'essaie." Il soupira et se retourna. "Je dois choisir moins de combats, car plus je perds, plus elle s'enhardit."

« Tu peux dire non, tu sais ? »

Mais il m'a juste jeté un regard comme si j'étais fou. "Je n'ai pas élevé cet enfant pour qu'il accepte un non comme réponse." Ah, c'est vrai.

Il me sourit, la malice derrière son regard. "Alors, tu lui as déjà donné?"

J'arquai un sourcil. — Pas encore, marmonnai-je, ne voulant pas que Banks m'entende.

"Puis-je compter sur vous pour une nuit calme ce soir, afin que je puisse profiter de ma femme?"

"Pourquoi me demandes tu?"

"Parce que toutes les vacances, la merde frappe le ventilateur à propos de quelque chose", ai-je aboyé.

Il plissa les yeux. « Thanksgiving n'était pas de ma faute.

"Le 4 juillet était de ta faute."

Il croisa les bras sur sa poitrine alors que les enfants finissaient d'allumer les bougies. "Et qui a donné à l'équipe de basket-ball de Thunder Bay les camions de votre oncle en mars dernier pour qu'ils puissent déverser du

39

fumier partout dans Falcon's Well après avoir perdu les championnats d'État?"

"Pas moi", ai-je rétorqué, creusant la saleté invisible sous mon ongle. « J'ai simplement oublié les clés. Je ne les ai donnés à personne. Il s'est moqué, les invités remplissant la salle autour de nous.

« En plus, nous n'avons pas perdu, lui dis-je. «Ils ont commis une faute. L'arbitre ne l'a tout simplement pas vu.

"Eh bien, la prochaine fois que vous 'laissez les clés dehors'", a-t-il dit en se mettant dans mon visage et en baissant la voix. "Souvenez-vous, ma femme était au téléphone avec leur maire, se faisant crier dessus pendant vingt-cinq minutes."

J'ai ouvert la bouche pour me défendre, mais rien n'est sorti. Ouais ok. Il avait raison. Ce n'était pas exactement juste, je suppose.

"Bien," dis-je.

Je me comporterais bien ce soir, mais j'attendais la même chose d'eux. Pas de drame.

Les habitants de la ville ont rempli la maison, certains masqués et d'autres maquillés, robes et bijoux scintillants à la lumière des bougies. J'ai fait une double prise, zonant leurs yeux pour voir qui je pouvais reconnaître dans leurs déguisements.

Quelques. Mais pas tout.

Quelque chose m'a mordu. Ce n'était plus intelligent. Les gens venaient d'entrer dans la maison. Personne ne vérifiait même les invitations.

Il n'y avait pas de sécurité autre que Lev, David et quelques autres circulant sur le terrain, et il n'y avait pas de gardes à la porte.

Nous n'avons pas provoqué d'ennuis, mais au fil des années, nous en avons acquis davantage. Plus de terres, plus de biens immobiliers, plus de pouvoir, plus d'argent... Et quand vous obtenez quelque chose qui en vaut la peine, quelqu'un finit par essayer de le prendre.

Nous avions eu de la chance jusqu'ici. Trop de chance.

« Nous sommes prêts ? » Em a appelé.

Mais avant que je puisse me retourner et répondre, une voix retentit depuis les escaliers. "'Lot 666, alors!'"

Emmy sursauta, se retourna, et tous nos yeux suivirent pour voir un homme avec une cape et un masque blanc couvrant la moitié de son visage.

"'Un lustre en morceaux!'"

41

Je ris, mettant mes inquiétudes de côté et reconnaissant Will instantanément. Michael secoua la tête, incapable de cacher son sourire.

Les enfants pouffèrent de rire alors que Will descendait les escaliers en faisant du jogging avec sa cape. « Certains d'entre vous se souviennent peut-être de l'étrange affaire du Fantôme du
Opéra.'"

"Papa !" J'ai ri.

Will a tourné en cercle, établissant un contact visuel avec tous les enfants. "'Un mystère jamais entièrement expliqué !'"

Et puis, au bon moment, l'orchestre et l'orgue remis à neuf au-dessus de nous ont entonné l'ouverture dramatique du Fantôme de l'Opéra, faisant à nouveau se dresser les cheveux sur mes bras.

Le sol vibra sous mes chaussures et mon pouls s'accéléra.

Winter ne pourrait pas sourire plus grand si elle essayait.

Quelqu'un a dû appuyer sur l'interrupteur, car le lustre a commencé à monter lentement, grimpant de plus en plus haut vers le plafond alors que nous inclinions la tête en arrière pour regarder.

Les flammes des bougies vacillaient avec le mouvement, et les enfants commencèrent à courir, virevolter et sauter dans la salle de bal.

Je les ai suivis, les invités s'infiltrant derrière moi, certains commençant à rejoindre Michael et Rika sur la piste de danse, tandis que d'autres arrachaient des coupes de champagne sur les plateaux des serveurs qui passaient.

Emmy a porté le bol de cendres de basilic, l'a posé sur la cheminée à côté de la menorah avant de marcher vers moi, son visage toujours illuminé.

Elle adorait allumer le lustre.

« Votre partie préférée… » pensai-je alors qu'elle s'installait à mes côtés, observant la pièce.

« Toujours », dit-elle en regardant au plafond les quatre petits appareils électriques au-dessus, qui ne sont pas utilisés actuellement. "J'aimerais presque qu'ils soient tous éclairés à la chandelle."

« Trop de travail », lui ai-je dit.

"Affirmative."

"Le clocher est magnifique." Je l'ai regardée. « J'adore ce que vous en avez fait. Ou refusé de s'en occuper, devrais-je dire.

Elle haussa les épaules. « Il y a de la beauté dans l'histoire. Je ne veux pas que cela soit effacé.

J'ai trouvé Banks sur la piste de danse, elle et Rika avec leurs têtes ensemble sur quelque chose.

« C'est là que je l'ai embrassée pour la première fois », ai-je dit en laissant mes yeux parcourir les épaules nues de ma femme.

"Je ne le savais pas."

"La nuit du diable." Le souvenir a joué dans ma tête. "Ma dernière année."

L'ouverture s'est terminée et le système audio a démarré, jouant une mélodie douce et obsédante avec des paroles.

Ensuite, Emmy a dit: "Elle était au confessionnal avec toi ce matin-là, n'est-ce pas?"

Je tournai mon regard vers elle. "Comment saviez-vous que?"

Elle sourit, comme si elle venait juste de se souvenir. « J'étais là ce jour-là. Je suis tombé sur elle.

"Tu vas à l'église ?" J'ai taquiné.

Mais elle se contenta de détourner le regard, un sourire timide aux lèvres. "J'avais mes raisons" Ou secrètes ? Peu importe. Ce n'est pas mes affaires.

« Le confessionnal », pensai-je. « C'était aussi la première fois que je lui parlais. Ce jour a changé ma vie.

"Le mien aussi."

"Si seulement je m'étais battu plus pour ce que je voulais." Cette journée s'est terminée bien pire qu'elle n'avait commencé. "Nous n'aurions pas manqué des années d'être ensemble."

"Moi aussi," ajouta-t-elle dans un murmure.

Banks me jetait des coups d'œil de temps en temps, ses lèvres rouges humides et ses yeux sombres. La chaleur couvrait mon corps alors que des images remplissaient ma tête de ce à quoi elle ressemblerait exactement avec ce maquillage pour le visage.

"Je dois danser avec elle", ai-je dit à Em et j'ai commencé à me déplacer sur le sol.

Mais alors une jeune brune était devant moi, les épaules nues dans une robe blanche.

"Kai," gazouilla-t-elle.

Je me suis arrêté, voyant mon élève très différente de celle qu'elle avait dans son cours d'aïkido les mardis et jeudis. "Soraya," dis-je, "Tu es superbe." Je pris sa main et me penchai, pressant ma joue contre sa tempe pour une rapide étreinte. « Vos parents sont-ils ici ?

"Non." Elle m'a souri. "Mais ils sont recroquevillés devant un feu ce soir."

"Bon à entendre."

J'ai essayé de la contourner et de lui dire au revoir, mais elle a recommencé à parler. "Merci pour les tête-à-tête de la semaine dernière", m'a-t-elle dit. "Ils ont vraiment aidé."

Elle me regarda avec des yeux bleus d'adoration, ses cheveux roux soyeux suspendus autour d'elle. Je pouvais presque sentir le sourire chargé d'Emmy à côté de moi.

S'il vous plaît. Le gamin était un… gamin.

"Bien sûr," lui ai-je dit. « Pratiquer une partie de la langue pendant les pauses ? »

"Ouais." Elle agrippa sa robe et je baissai les yeux, la regardant soulever lentement l'ourlet du sol. "Je l'emporte partout avec moi."

Alors que la robe montait de plus en plus haut, j'ai vu des marques noires dériver sur la peau dorée de sa jambe.

"Ichi, ni, san", récita-t-elle, lisant les chiffres japonais comme une feuille de triche sur son corps.

"Yon, vas-y, roku." Elle souleva la robe plus haut, au-dessus de son genou et jusqu'à sa cuisse. "Nana, hachi..."

La sueur me rafraîchit le front et je jetai un coup d'œil à Banks, la voyant nous regarder avec ses yeux en feu.

"Merde," articulai-je en voyant Emmy cacher son sourire avec sa main.

"Ku." Soraya continua, la robe sur le point de remonter jusqu'à elle… "Juu," dit-elle finalement.

J'ai dégluti, mes yeux revenant à Banks, Rika debout à côté d'elle, les yeux écarquillés et presque prête à rire.

J'ai aperçu les gars qui me regardaient aussi, leurs lèvres bougeant, et même si je ne comprenais pas ce qu'ils disaient, je pouvais lire leurs sourires de merde.

Je baissais à nouveau les yeux, essayant de ne pas voir la longue jambe de Soraya. "C'est... c'est bien."

Elle laissa retomber la robe. "Je sais que le dojo est fermé jusqu'après le nouvel an, mais j'ai laissé mon sac dans le vestiaire." Elle s'est rapprochée et j'ai reculé d'un pas. « Serez-vous présent ce week-end ? Comme pour la paperasse ou autre ? Je peux

47

m'arrêter. Juste très rapide. Seul? Pendant que je suis là-dedans... seul ?

J'ai jeté mes yeux sur Banks, et en même temps, elle et Rika ont passé leurs doigts sur leur gorge en signe de menace.

Emmy renifla, attrapant une coupe de champagne sur un plateau qui passait. « J'ai déjà vu ça. Tel frère, telles sœurs. »

*Nom de Dieu.*Ce n'était pas ma faute. Banks allait être énervé toute la nuit maintenant.

J'ai esquivé la fille. «Ma femme sera là toute la journée demain, s'occupant de certaines choses», lui ai-je dit. "Je lui ferai savoir que vous passez." Et je me suis foutu de là.

Mais alors que j'essayais de me diriger vers Banks, les gars ont plongé, m'interrompant.

"Quelqu'un a des ennuis", taquina Will.

"Laisse-moi tranquille." L'enfant a le béguin. Comme si je pouvais le contrôler.

J'ai essayé de chercher ma femme, mais les danseurs tournaient et je ne pouvais pas voir autour des gars.

"Merde," marmonnai-je en glissant mes mains dans mes poches.

"Ouais", a ajouté Michael. "Tout le monde a vu ça."

"Ta gueule."

"Oh merde." Damon rit dans sa barbe en portant son verre à ses lèvres. "Voilà les gants."

Hein? J'ai retrouvé Banks alors que Rika essayait de retenir son rire, parlant clairement à Banks alors que ma femme lançait des regards noirs à l'adolescente.

"Voir!" Je me suis tourné vers Michel. « Qu'est-ce que je t'ai dit ? La merde frappe toujours le ventilateur.

« Détendez-vous », me dit-il. « Banks vous fait confiance. Alors la reine adolescente a le béguin pour son maître sensei.

"Sa tutelle a marqué tout autour de ses cuisses..." railla Damon.

"Et ma femme a des couteaux enroulés autour de la sienne", chuchotai-je, conscient de nos invités. "Merde. Regarde-les." Je fis signe aux filles, Winter et Emory les ayant rejointes. "Ils préparent quelque chose." Will et Michael pouffèrent de rire, ne bougeant pas d'un pouce pour arrêter quoi que ce soit.

"Je suis plus inquiet pour cette jeune fille que pour toi," songea Damon.

J'étais plus inquiet pour la nuit où j'avais prévu d'aller en enfer. Ma femme me faisait confiance, mais ça l'énervait vraiment quand les autres femmes ne se souciaient toujours pas que j'étais marié. Non pas que cela arrivait souvent, mais elle y voyait le signe du plus ultime manque de respect. De cette façon, elle et Damon ressemblaient plus à leur père qu'ils ne l'admettraient jamais.

"Éloignez-la de ma femme enceinte, s'il vous plaît", a déclaré Michael. « Elle ressemble à une bombe. Ouais.

J'ai commencé à m'éloigner, mais Jett a couru vers moi et m'a sauté dans les bras. Je l'ai attrapée juste à temps.

"Papa, on va au théâtre maintenant !" elle a annoncé.

« Vous avez tout le monde ? Michael a demandé à Miss Englestat, qui a trouvé Dag et Fane dans chaque main.

"Oui, monsieur," lui dit-elle, à bout de souffle. « Athos reste derrière, et Mme Cuthbert a des onglets sur Madden et Octavia. Tous les autres sont comptabilisés.

Les garçons de Damon se sont accrochés pour un câlin, mais Ivarsen est passé en coup de vent, ses pouces tapotant sur son téléphone.

"Hé, sois sage," l'appela Damon.

"À tout", a terminé le gamin pour lui.

J'ai ri. Arbre? Rencontrez la pomme.

"Bonne chasse." J'ai embrassé ma fille sur le nez et je l'ai serrée contre moi.

"Rendez-vous à minuit."

Mais elle a commencé à donner des coups. « Laissez-moi partir ou Indie prendra ma place ! »

Je l'ai laissé tomber au sol. "Sois sage."

Sans un mot de plus, elle se précipita vers le hall, l'une des nounous enroulant son manteau autour d'elle.

Alors que les enfants partaient pour les prochaines heures – prêts à rejoindre le reste des enfants en ville pour des friandises et des festivités au théâtre – la musique est devenue un peu plus dure et plus profonde, et j'ai de nouveau cherché Banks dans la foule.

Mais mon regard a attrapé quelque chose pendant que je regardais. Quelqu'un me regardait.

Masque entièrement blanc. Cape noire. Près de la cheminée. Je cligne des yeux et me retourne, essayant de retrouver son visage alors que mon pouls saute un battement.

Qui-?

51

Aucun des hommes ne portait de cape. Maintenant, ce serait trop habillé.

Mais quand je l'ai cherché à nouveau, il n'était pas là. Un frisson me parcourut le dos à la façon dont il venait de se tenir là, les creux noirs de ses yeux figés sur moi.

"Tu ferais mieux d'y aller," dit Damon.

Hein?

Je me tournai vers lui, le voyant faire un geste derrière moi. Suivant son regard, j'ai finalement aperçu ma femme alors qu'elle enfilait un demi-masque blanc, couvrant ses yeux et son nez, me regardant alors qu'elle reculait lentement dans l'ombre. J'ai fléchi ma mâchoire alors même que mon aine se gonflait de chaleur à quel point elle était narquoise.

N'ose pas.

Je partis, la suivant, l'homme au manteau et au masque oubliés.

J'évitai les danseurs, me faufilant dans la foule, l'atteignant juste à temps pour lui prendre le bras.

« Arrête », lui ai-je murmuré à l'oreille.

Elle se tendit, refusant de se retourner et de me faire face.

"Je n'allais pas la tuer," dit-elle à voix basse, fixant la jeune Soraya au bord de la pièce. "Faites-lui juste un peu peur."

"C'est une enfant."

"Oui." Elle tourna la tête, me défiant. "Je crois me souvenir que j'avais l'âge de cet enfant la première fois que tu as mis ta main sous ma chemise."

Le souvenir de cette fille mystérieuse dans mes bras dans le clocher m'envahit à nouveau. "Votre chemise," lui fis-je remarquer.

Pas la sienne.

Elle se retourna, ses yeux verts et son maquillage pour les yeux me transperçant à travers le masque blanc. "Je le pense," dit-elle, s'éloignant comme si elle était quelque chose que je ne pourrais jamais avoir. "Tu ne tolérerais pas que j'enseigne à quelqu'un qui a flirté avec moi."

"Et tu ne me laisserais pas dicter ce que tu es autorisé et non autorisé à faire." Je m'avançai alors qu'elle reculait. J'admettrais que j'aimais bien sa jalousie.

Mais alors je ne l'ai pas fait.

Je n'aimais pas que cela puisse venir de l'insécurité.

"Tu ne lui fais pas confiance ?" Je lui ai demandé.

"Quoi?"

"Que cela ne finira jamais."

Elle avait besoin que tout le monde sache que j'étais à elle, alors que cela lui éviterait beaucoup d'agacement si cela pouvait être suffisant de savoir que je savais que j'étais à elle.

Je me dirigeai vers elle, pas lent après pas lent alors que mes yeux tombaient sur ses seins menaçant de sauter par-dessus sa robe.

Et croyez-moi, je savais que j'étais à elle.

L'homme dans son lit tous les soirs. Le père de ses enfants. Son partenaire dans tout ce que j'ai fait.

« Je veux te donner quelque chose », lui ai-je dit.

Des couples tourbillonnaient autour de nous, aucun de nous ne clignant des yeux alors que ses yeux semblaient briller dans la pénombre.

"Viens ici maintenant," dis-je.

Mais elle ne l'a pas fait. Elle n'arrêtait pas de reculer.

Mon sang s'est mis à bouillir. Nous n'avons pas eu toute la nuit. Il y avait des trucs que je voulais faire avant le retour des enfants. "Tu me fais chier," ai-je mordu, creuser dans mes talons. "Tu sais que je n'aime pas faire des scènes." Mais je le ferais s'il le fallait.

Elle ne m'a pas donné de chance. Dès qu'elle atteignit le bord de la pièce, elle se retourna, plongea à travers les doubles portes et disparut. Je me suis précipité après elle, ne me souciant pas des yeux que j'ai surpris en train de clignoter dans notre direction.

En entrant dans la pièce voisine, sombre avec seulement un couple caché dans le coin en train de s'embrasser, j'ai aperçu sa robe rouge alors qu'elle disparaissait dans un autre coin. Je l'ai poursuivie, la voyant finalement se précipiter dans la cage d'escalier arrière.

Courant après elle, je contournai l'escalier en colimaçon, les pierres grinçaient sous ma chaussure.

Juste au moment où nous atteignions le deuxième étage et qu'elle essayait de s'échapper jusqu'au troisième, je lui ai attrapé le bras et l'ai fouettée, la clouant au mur.

"Comme si je ne t'attraperais pas," me moquai-je. "Je ne sais même pas pourquoi tu essaies."

Un cierge scintillait sur le mur, et je la regardai dans les yeux, mes lèvres planant sur les siennes.

Elle bascula contre le mur, mais je la repoussai et remontai sa robe, pressant ma main entre ses jambes, mes doigts en feu alors que je la frottais doucement.

Jésus Christ. Elle était nue. Complètement nu.

Elle frissonna mais cessa de se battre, et je souris, adorant ces petites surprises rares qu'elle me faisait.

Aucune culotte ne lui ressemblait autant.

"Qu'est-ce que vous et les filles planifiiez là-bas?" murmurai-je par-dessus sa bouche.

"N—Rien."

Je glissai ma main à l'intérieur de ses cuisses, sentant ma bite durcir. Dieu, je ne pouvais pas attendre.

"Regarde-moi, Nik."

Lentement, ses yeux se sont levés, incapables de me résister quand j'ai utilisé son vrai nom.

« Je veux te donner quelque chose », ai-je dit, la bouche sèche de besoin. « Atteignez ma veste. Sors-le."

Je fis courir mes doigts sur sa peau douce, puis mes jointures, ayant besoin que chaque centimètre de ma peau touche chaque centimètre de la sienne.

Elle fouilla dans ma poche de poitrine et en sortit un mouchoir, enroulé autour d'un petit objet.

J'ai arrêté de la frotter, mais je n'ai pas bougé la main pendant qu'elle déballait le cadeau.

Un peigne en argent posé à l'intérieur du tissu, le motif orné de trois rubis brillant vers elle.

« C'était celui de ma mère », lui ai-je dit.

« Et celui de sa mère.

C'était l'une des seules choses que ma mère avait laissées de sa famille. Ma grand-mère avait dû le lui passer en contrebande après s'être enfuie avec mon père.

Ses yeux se posèrent sur les miens, et j'espérai qu'elle comprenait ce que signifiait l'héritage.

« Les femmes de ma famille le transmettent à leurs filles », expliquai-je.

"Ma mère voulait te l'offrir elle-même, mais elle le savait..."

Je ne pouvais pas forcer les mots, mais ses yeux se sont baissés, son menton tremblant. Elle savait ce que j'allais dire.

Banks n'avait pas reçu beaucoup de cadeaux des autres dans la vie, et aucun de ses propres parents. Cela la rendait encore nerveuse. Ma mère savait que ce serait peut-être plus facile venant de moi.

Levant les mains, elle ajusta le peigne à l'arrière de ses cheveux et enroula ses bras autour de moi.

Son nez effleura le mien. "Je veux tuer n'importe qui pour avoir essayé de t'éloigner de moi."

J'ai passé mes mains autour de ses fesses, sentant la sangle de lames autour de sa jambe, et je l'ai soulevée dans mes bras. "Si jamais je te quitte, c'est parce que je suis mort."

J'enfonçai ma bouche dans la sienne, prouvant la seule assurance dont elle aurait jamais besoin, et je le ferais cent fois par jour pour le reste de ma vie si elle en avait besoin.

Elle n'avait jamais rien eu à craindre de perdre dans la vie, et j'allais me casser le dos pour tout lui donner.

Dieu, elle était incroyable.

J'ai ouvert mon pantalon, je suis sorti et je me suis installé à l'intérieur d'elle, poussant en elle juste là dans la cage d'escalier sombre.

"Ah," gémit-elle, s'accrochant à sa vie. "Je t'aime, Kaï."

"Je t'aime aussi," soufflai-je à travers sa bouche. « Je ne peux pas m'arrêter. Je ne veux plus jamais m'arrêter."

J'ai pompé en elle fort et vite, frénétique, alors que j'enfouis mon visage dans son cou et qu'elle me serra dans ses bras.

J'ai enregistré un cri ou quelque chose quelque part au loin, puis des hurlements d'en bas.

« Kai », gémit-elle en me ramenant. "Je pense que j'entends des cris."

*On s'en fout?*Je m'en foutais. Toute la maison pourrait être en feu en ce moment, et je m'en fiche.

Je la regardai dans les yeux. Un camion devrait me traîner loin de toi.

59

Damon

Eh bien, c'est nouveau.

Un putain de cheval noir trottait dans la salle de bal, un cavalier masqué portant une cape nous surplombant alors que la musique s'arrêtait, la danse s'arrêtait et tout le monde reculait, lui laissant amplement d'espace.

J'attrapai Octavia, la tirant avec moi. "Viens ici."

Quelques cris ont frappé l'air, tandis que d'autres ont haleté et se sont moqués de l'affichage.

Qu'est-ce que c'était? Je veux dire, je n'ai pas prêté attention aux détails, mais je me serais souvenu que Michael et Rika avaient mentionné un énorme mammifère chevauchant dans leur maison dans le cadre des festivités.

Putain d'Athos. Cela puait Edgar Allan Poe.

Le cavalier portait un masque de crâne et j'ai poussé Tavi dans mes bras, la regardant le regarder, ses yeux brillant d'excitation.

Le cheval s'est arrêté, tout le monde s'est calmé et a attendu avec impatience, et l'air frais qu'il a apporté avec lui a refroidi ma peau.

"Le fantôme regarde depuis la case cinq", a-t-il tonné, sa voix résonnant. "Vous le verrez, bien qu'il ne soit pas vivant."

Octavia ne bougea pas un muscle, tout le monde autour utilisant son téléphone pour filmer son message.

« Apportez-moi son masque à la lueur du feu de joie ! cria-t-il, tournant en cercle pour atteindre les oreilles de tout le monde. "Votre trésor vous attend avant la fin de Fire Night."

Et puis, il s'élança, quittant la pièce, les sabots du cheval claquant contre le sol de marbre. Au bout d'un moment, nous avons entendu les galops rapides alors qu'il s'éloignait dans la nuit.

Je ris en regardant le visage d'Octavia, qui était toujours impressionnée. Ces enfants allaient avoir un réveil brutal lorsqu'ils sont arrivés au monde et ont réalisé qu'il n'y avait pas d'endroit comme Thunder Bay.

Mais ça allait. Si j'avais tout ce qu'il fallait, ils n'auraient jamais à découvrir à quel point le reste du monde était nul par rapport à chez eux.

"Boîte cinq?" quelqu'un a dit. « Alors, le théâtre, alors ?

Les gens se déplaçaient, les bavardages envahissant la pièce alors que les plus jeunes commençaient à partir, rassemblant leurs manteaux et déchiffrant ses indices pour la chasse au trésor.

"Peut-être l'intrigue cinq?" une autre personne a ajouté. « Au cimetière ? L'énigme disait que le fantôme n'était pas vivant, alors... »

« Serait-ce une tombe ? une autre femme intervint.

"Mais il 'regarde'", a soutenu un autre, rejouant le message sur son téléphone. "Une statue? Situé d'un point de vue, peut-être ? »

Les invités filtraient hors de la pièce, les plus jeunes se précipitant dans la nuit pour essayer d'être les premiers à gagner le million de dollars en fiducie qu'ils pourraient utiliser pour l'université ou - puisque beaucoup avaient déjà payé l'université - ils pourraient y accéder une fois diplômés , dont la plupart l'utiliseraient pour voyager, investir ou créer leur propre entreprise.

Environ la moitié des invités restèrent, la musique, la danse et les conversations recommencèrent alors que je déposais Octavia et lui tenais les mains, se balançant avec elle.

« Pourquoi ne puis-je pas y aller ce soir ? » elle a demandé.

"Parce que notre famille organise la chasse." Je la regardai alors qu'elle enfilait mes chaussures et me laissait conduire. "Ce ne serait pas juste si nous le gagnions, n'est-ce pas?"

"Ce n'est pas juste de toute façon." Vous faites la moue ?

Je baissai les yeux, amusé. "Le jour de votre anniversaire, recevez-vous des cadeaux ou en donnez-vous?" Quand elle ne répondait pas, je répondais à sa place. « C'est la même différence. La chasse est un cadeau de notre part pour la ville. Il y a d'autres trésors pour vous là-bas.

J'ai regardé, voyant Christiane trébucher alors qu'elle essayait de danser avec son mari, Matthew, son comportement pathétique aussi superbement fantastique que l'attitude stupide de son fils. Je veux dire, à quoi pensait-elle, l'épouser ? Il avait à peine le courage de gérer une phrase. Il était silencieux. Elle était calme. Cette maison doit être une fête tous les jours. Comment ont-ils décidé quand avoir des relations sexuelles ? Par texto ?

Et puis une image d'eux en train de faire l'amour a envahi mon cerveau, et j'ai retenu le grognement avant qu'il ne s'échappe.

"Où sont-elles?" J'ai entendu Octavia demander.

Je clignai des yeux, me retournant vers elle. « Où est quoi ? »

"Mes trésors."

« Tu dois les trouver », lui ai-je dit. « Et combats pour eux. Rien n'est donné. »

Ses lèvres se sont tordues sur le côté et j'ai failli rire. Je voulais qu'elle rêve, mais c'était là que les rêves étaient dangereux. Rien ne s'est jamais passé comme vous le vouliez. Cela allait être plus difficile qu'elle ne le pensait, et elle échouerait plusieurs fois avant de gagner. C'était ce qu'elle ne savait pas encore.

Ce n'est pas le combat qui t'a eu. C'était le leurre qu'on pouvait toujours abandonner.

Elle aurait besoin d'un peu d'entraînement.

J'ai arrêté de danser et j'ai fouillé dans ma poche de poitrine, lui tendant le parchemin que j'avais préparé. "J'avais le sentiment que tu bouderais."

Elle prit le papier plié et l'ouvrit, son vernis à ongles noir ébréché alors qu'elle prenait mon cadeau pour elle.

Elle haleta. "Une carte au trésor !"

J'ai pointé du doigt. « C'est quelque part dans cette maison. Dessus de nous."

Elle fit le tour de la pièce du regard, inclinant finalement la tête en arrière et fixant la balustrade de la galerie sombre au deuxième étage.

"Puis-je avoir de l'aide?" elle me demanda.

Nous ne pouvions voir personne, mais nous savions qui était là-haut, et je savais à qui elle faisait référence.

J'ai hoché la tête. "Mmm, allez-y."

Je mettrais quelques mots sur la carte qu'elle aurait peut-être besoin d'aide pour lire de toute façon.

Elle a commencé à s'enfuir, mais elle a heurté quelqu'un, et je me suis déplacé pour la rattraper, mais il était loin devant moi. Il attrapa ses épaules et la redressa avant de se redresser.

J'ai levé les yeux, voyant un homme portant un masque blanc et une cape reculer, la regarder, puis s'incliner dramatiquement.

— Madame, dit-il.

"Désolé," gazouilla-t-elle.

Et puis elle s'est enfuie, se dirigeant vers l'escalier pour aller chercher sa cousine. Je ris, hochant la tête vers l'homme qui passait, et reconnaissant que mon enfant était dur mais aussi poli.

Je le regardai, remarquant la cape. Un peu trop habillé, mais bon.

J'ai jeté un coup d'œil à l'étage, voyant une ombre passer le plafond alors que Tavi courait vers Madden.

Il se cachait toujours pendant des fonctions comme celle-ci. Kai a essayé d'expliquer qu'il était mal à l'aise dans les situations sociales, mais je pense que c'était une courtoisie de la part de Mads. Les invités étaient mal à l'aise quand il était là.

Glissant mes mains dans mes poches, je me promenai dans la pièce, regardant ma femme alors qu'elle dansait avec le père de Kai, sa femme en pleine conversation avec quelques dames du club de jardinage. J'ai croisé les yeux de Rika alors qu'elle se tenait près de la cheminée, mâchonnant un autre macaron au thé vert.

Elle se figea en me voyant la regarder. J'arquai un sourcil. Un autre? Vous voulez aussi un gâteau ? Peut-être deux gâteaux, Rika ? Elle n'hésita qu'un instant et le fourra dans sa bouche, suivi d'un autre, avant de me retourner et de s'éloigner avec ses joues de tamia pleines d'aliments malsains pour le bébé.

J'ai ri, juste pour la taquiner. Winter avait aussi eu ses envies. Profitez au maximum.

Je regardai ma femme, l'aimant plus que tout à cette période de l'année. Elle adorait la musique, la nourriture et toutes les petites choses. Elle ne pouvait pas voir les lumières, mais d'une certaine manière, elle les voyait. Elle a dit qu'ils rendaient la maison différente. Plus chaud, en quelque sorte.

J'ai adoré que rien ne lui échappe. Même l'odeur du papier d'emballage. Il ne m'était jamais venu à l'esprit que le papier d'emballage avait une odeur, mais elle m'obligeait à m'allonger sous le sapin chaque hiver et à inhaler les cadeaux.

Elle avait raison. Je l'ai remarqué maintenant.

Kai et Banks retournèrent dans la salle de bal de là où ils s'étaient cachés, les cheveux de Banks pendaient maintenant autour d'elle alors que Kai rajustait sa cravate. Will a fait tournoyer Emmy sur la piste de danse désormais spacieuse, puisque certains des invités étaient partis, son rire remplissant la pièce.

Mais ensuite j'ai vu Matthew se diriger à travers la pièce, à travers le hall central, dans la salle à manger.

Christiane n'était pas avec lui. Je l'ai immédiatement cherchée.

La repérant alors qu'elle dérivait dans la direction opposée, j'hésitai un instant, la regardant disparaître dans la pièce voisine. Je me suis tendu, quelque chose me mordillant comme ça l'a fait de plus en plus ces deux dernières années.

Au cours des jours, des mois et des décennies qui se sont écoulés depuis que j'ai découvert que la mère de Rika était aussi la mienne, j'ai attendu ce que j'étais sûr de venir d'elle.

Échec.

À un moment donné, elle rechuterait. Elle oublierait un de mes enfants au magasin ou au parc. La nouveauté d'être une grand-mère aimante, attentive et responsable se dissiperait ou prendrait trop d'énergie pour suivre le rythme, et elle disparaîtrait lentement de nos vies.

Peu importe à quel point je pouvais être froide, ou les années passées à lui répondre en un seul mot, rien ne l'avait déconcertée, cependant. Elle n'était rien, sinon patiente.

Au fil du temps, le contraire s'est produit. Au lieu d'abandonner, mon combat a commencé à s'essouffler. Il était difficile de ne pas aimer à quel point elle était indulgente avec Octavia – confectionnant presque tous ses vêtements à la main, car il n'y avait vraiment aucun vêtement d'époque de qualité dans le style que Tavi aimait qui ne ressemblait à un costume bon marché.

Elle était incroyable avec Gunnar, toujours réfléchie dans les ventes de garage pour les pièces de rechange qu'il pourrait utiliser pour ses inventions, et cela ne la dérangeait pas quand Fane et Dag détruisaient sa maison, construisant des forts dans chaque pièce.

Elle avait été d'une grande aide lorsque Winter était à l'hôpital pour donner naissance à Octavia, l'un des chiens de Kai avait presque mordu l'oreille d'Ivarsen et il n'avait que six ans. Elle est restée dans la chambre d'hôpital avec lui deux étages plus bas quand je devais être avec Winter.

Je ne voulais pas ravaler ma fierté. J'avais l'impression d'étouffer.

Mais de plus en plus, je commençais aussi à détester la douleur dans ses yeux qu'elle essayait de dissimuler quand je l'ignorais. Je m'en foutais.

Quelque chose avait changé.

Je la suivis, mes pieds bougeant sans réfléchir.

Ouvrant la porte blanche, je me glissai dans la pièce voisine, une salle de bal plus petite, sombre et vide. Elle se tenait à la fenêtre, le clair de lune faisant scintiller sa robe blanche scintillante et ses cheveux blonds tirés en chignon.

Je suis resté là, fermant la porte derrière moi en la regardant.

C'était comme si elle attendait quelque chose.

"Tu fais ça beaucoup." Je croisai les bras sur ma poitrine. "Laissez des pièces pleines de monde pour être seul."

Elle ne se retourna pas, se contentant de serrer les mains devant elle.

"Je le fais pour vous donner l'occasion de me suivre", a-t-elle déclaré. "Je pensais que tu ne me parlerais pas avec d'autres autour."

"Tu penses que tu me connais?"

Elle tourna la tête, rencontrant mon regard. "Tu ne me connais pas." Sa voix s'adoucit. « Il y a tellement de choses que je dois dire. J'attendais de dire.

Je n'ai pas bougé. Eh bien, écoutons-le, alors. Vous avez eu des années pour vous préparer.

Une partie de moi mourait d'envie d'entendre cela, ne serait-ce que pour rouvrir de vieilles blessures et me mettre à nouveau en colère. Assez en colère pour me rappeler pourquoi je devrais la détester.

Elle m'avait abandonné. Chaque jour, pendant des années.

Elle était peut-être une bonne personne, mais était-ce important ? Avais-je besoin d'elle maintenant ?

Non.

Elle tourna son corps mais resta à sa place. « Vous souvenez-vous de l'ours en peluche que j'ai offert à Ivarsen lors de son premier Noël ? Je n'ai toujours pas bougé. Ou répondre.

Mais je m'en suis souvenu. Il était petit, environ la moitié de sa taille, avec un ruban rouge noué autour du cou. Il avait été enveloppé dans du vieux papier brun froissé avec un nœud poussiéreux. Je me souvenais avoir pensé qu'il n'avait pas l'air à sa place parmi les sacs et les boîtes de fantaisie des autres cadeaux qu'elle lui avait achetés.

Elle a baissé les yeux et j'ai commencé à me tendre.

Eh bien, quoi? L'a-t-elle volé alors qu'elle était défoncée ? Tu veux dire le donner à Madden ? Quoi?

« Cet ours était à toi », m'a-t-elle dit. "C'était à toi depuis que tu étais bébé."

Je serrai la mâchoire.

Je l'entendis déglutir, mais elle ne s'approcha pas. « J'ai pensé que je trouverais un moyen de vous le faire parvenir, ainsi que tous les autres cadeaux que j'ai achetés au cours de la

Des Noëls et des
anniversaires
au fil des
années. Je la
fixai sans
cligner des
yeux.

73

"La boîte à musique que j'ai donnée à Octavia, les camions jouets que j'ai donnés à Fane, et le bateau télécommandé et les livres que j'ai donnés à Dag et Gunnar..."

Ma gorge s'est enflée et j'ai essayé d'enfoncer les aiguilles, mais je n'ai pas pu.

Tout à moi. Une image de tous les jouets emballés, ramassant la poussière dans son grenier et attendant un enfant qui ne les ouvrirait jamais m'a traversé la tête, mais je l'ai repoussée.

Et alors? J'avais tous les jouets dont je pouvais rêver en grandissant. Je ne suis jamais allé sans quoi que ce soit que l'argent puisse acheter. Je ne l'ai pas manqué.

"C'est de ma faute." Elle fit un pas vers moi. « Tout ce avec quoi... tout ce avec quoi tu as grandi, ce n'est pas de ta faute. Ce n'est même pas le leur. Elle secoua la tête. «Ce n'étaient pas de bonnes personnes. Nous ne pouvions pas nous attendre à ce qu'ils fassent de bonnes choses, mais j'étais une bonne personne autrefois, et même si je ne savais pas à quel point c'était mauvais pour toi, je savais que ce n'était pas bon. Je serrai les poings sous mes bras.

Elle a de nouveau baissé les yeux et j'ai vu quelque chose de brillant tomber sur sa joue.

"Je voulais mourir." Sa voix était épaisse de larmes. « Je méritais de mourir. J'essayais de mourir.

Chaque muscle de mon corps s'est durci.

"Mon Dieu, je voulais que tout se termine", murmura-t-elle, les épaules tremblantes. "Je n'avais aucune idée à quel point le monde pouvait être laid jusqu'à ton père."

Elle est devenue floue dans ma vision, parce que c'était une bonne façon de le dire. Avec mon père, tout était sombre et infernal.

"J'étais un enfant." Elle s'approcha. « Je ne savais même pas faire du vélo jusqu'à l'âge de dix-huit ans. Schraeder m'a appris. J'étais tellement à l'abri.

Des larmes ont coulé sur son visage en pensant à cette adolescente, plus jeune que Rika quand je l'ai terrorisée.

Banks, Winter, Em, Rika… Je ne doutais pas qu'ils survivraient à ce que Christiane avait traversé, mais… ils auraient été blessés. Gravement blessé, à l'intérieur comme à l'extérieur.

La colère me tordait les tripes rien que d'y penser.

"Rika a été si seule pendant si longtemps," murmura-t-elle. « Silencieuse, douce, pressant toujours son nez contre la vitre, essayant de voir dans un monde dans lequel elle attendait d'être invitée. Elle n'avait pas de voix, parce que je n'en avais pas à lui donner.

Je me suis souvenu.

"Les années se sont estompées", a-t-elle poursuivi, "et tout moment de clarté était comme un couteau dans mon cerveau. Je ne pouvais pas le prendre. Je ne supportais pas de me souvenir de toi. J'étais si faible.

Je savais ce que c'était. J'avais des cicatrices pour le prouver. Elle avait des pilules. J'avais des lames de rasoir.

Mais ce n'était pas une faiblesse pour moi.

C'était faire face. J'avais quelque chose à faire.

"Mais elle a fini par trouver son chemin, n'est-ce pas ?" demanda-t-elle sans attendre de réponse. « Michael, Kai Mori, Will Grayson… vous. J'aurais dû savoir que la vie trouverait un moyen de prendre soin d'elle quand j'ai échoué. J'aurais dû savoir que vous vous retrouveriez. Un doux sourire passa sur ses lèvres. « Elle parle comme si elle avait dix mille soldats derrière elle maintenant. Tu as fait ça. Pas moi."

Rika a appris tout ce qu'elle ne voulait pas être en voyant chaque jour à quoi ressemble une vie gâchée, tout comme Banks et moi l'avons fait dans ma maison.

« Et tu es heureux », me dit-elle. « L'hiver a fait ça. Pas moi."

Christiane avait enfin appris ce qu'elle aurait dû enseigner à ses enfants – au lieu qu'ils lui apprennent – vous êtes à cent pour cent responsable de votre propre bonheur.

« Je suis reconnaissante que les leçons qu'elle a apprises n'aient pas coûté trop cher », dit-elle en s'approchant de moi. "Et je regrette à jamais que le vôtre ait atteint autant." Son menton tremblait. "Je suis désolé. Mon Dieu, j'aimerais pouvoir revenir en arrière et tout faire différemment. Je ferais tout différemment, même s'il me tuait pour ça.

J'ai forcé la boule dans ma gorge, ma tête me faisant mal, essayant de retenir mes larmes.

Il l'aurait tuée. Elle aurait peut-être dû se battre. J'aurais dû essayer. J'aurais dû me préparer quand j'étais assez vieux pour approcher, ou obtenir de l'aide de personnes que mon père craignait, mais peut-être que ça se serait quand même mal terminé, et au lieu d'avoir une mère malade, Rika et moi aurions fini par sans un.

Assez de temps avait été perdu.

"Je serai toujours désolée, mais j'avais besoin que tu saches que je t'aime", a-t-elle déclaré. « Toujours, et il y a un cadeau de plus sous cet arbre là-bas que ces beaux enfants ne peuvent pas avoir, parce que c'était toujours le tien. Vous pouvez l'ouvrir après mon départ ou jamais du tout, mais je devais vous le donner.

Elle a commencé à partir, toujours en s'esquivant, parce qu'elle ne voulait pas prolonger son accueil, mais alors que j'étais curieux de savoir ce qu'elle avait pour moi quand j'étais enfant qu'elle a laissé sous l'arbre, je ne voulais pas qu'elle parte pourtant non plus.

– Christiane, ai-je dit.

Elle s'arrêta et je la regardai à côté de moi, pas sûr d'avoir l'estomac pour ça. Je ne faisais pas confiance aux parents et j'étais trop vieux pour commencer.

Mais je ne voulais plus lui faire de mal.

Peut-être que je pourrais être son fils, éventuellement. Peut être pas.

Mais on pourrait essayer d'être quelque chose.

« Comment se fait-il que vous ne sachiez pas danser ? J'ai demandé.

Elle cligna des yeux. Elle et Matthew ressemblaient à deux collégiens lors de leur premier Spring Fling là-bas. Je pensais qu'elle était cultivée.

Elle bougea, l'air incertain. "Je ne sais pas grand-chose, je suppose."

Le bourdonnement sourd de la musique traversait les murs, mais j'ai pu distinguer la mélodie en me tournant vers elle.

Tendre ma main, j'ai attendu pendant qu'elle me regardait, l'air un peu choqué.

Enfin, elle s'est emparée. Je l'attirai à moi, sa main fraîche s'emboîtant dans la mienne tandis que je glissais l'autre autour de sa taille. Mon cœur rata un battement, sentant ma mère dans mes bras pour la première fois.

Elle a levé les yeux vers moi, les rides autour de ses yeux révélant son âge, mais le regard en eux ressemblait toujours à celui d'un enfant.

« Suivez mon exemple », ai-je ordonné.

Poussant, je l'ai déplacée dans la pièce vide, la musique à peine audible alors que nous tournions et marchions. Je la regardai, quelque chose enflait dans ma gorge, et ça me faisait mal, mais je ne pouvais pas non plus détourner le regard.

Je n'avais pas besoin d'elle. J'avais fait une belle famille, pas seulement ma femme et mes enfants, mais aussi mes amis. J'avais tout.

Et pourtant, en la tenant dans mes bras, j'ai réalisé quelque chose qui manquait. J'ai réalisé à quel point je voulais la rapprocher et m'accrocher à quelque chose.

Parfois, j'étais tellement fatigué. Je pourrais demander de l'aide, m'appuyer sur les gars ou me défouler sur les femmes, mais je ne le ferais pas. Jamais.

Je voulais être fort pour eux. Je n'ai jamais voulu que Banks me voie à nouveau effrayé, ou que Rika me voie perdre ma merde et ne pas être capable de gérer quelque chose.

Je n'ai jamais voulu que mes enfants me voient moins qu'un homme.

Je ne savais pas trop pourquoi, mais avec Christiane, je me fichais de ne pas être la plus forte de la pièce. Même dans la trentaine, je devais admettre que je voulais toujours une maman.

Une maman pourrait être là pour les moments où vous étiez vulnérable.

L'attirant plus près, je la portai sur le sol, l'entendant émettre un rire alors que nous tournions, ses pieds touchant à peine le sol à mesure que je bougeais plus vite.

Comme c'était étrange d'être parent. Pendant tant d'années, je ne me voyais pas à sa place, et même si je savais que je ferais tant de choses différemment si j'avais été elle, je pouvais au moins comprendre à quel point il était probablement difficile d'être désespéré pour votre enfant et regarder une autre femme l'élever.

Entre Christiane, Natalya et Gabriel, ils ont tout fait de travers.

Mais j'étais toujours là.

Banks était toujours là. Rika était toujours là. Malgré tout, nous avons survécu à nos parents.

Pas une seule fois Banks ou Rika ne leur avaient reproché quoi que ce soit. Je n'avais rien fait d'autre que blâmer Christiane au cours de la dernière décennie.

Avec quelle facilité mes propres enfants pourraient-ils faire demi-tour et faire de même ? Tout cet amour que j'avais pour eux, et ils pouvaient encore me détester.

J'ai ralenti mes pieds, un poids s'est posé sur mes épaules, et j'étais si fatigué tout d'un coup.

Et effrayé. Elle voulait être plus, mais elle a échoué. Comment ai-je su que je ne le ferais pas ? Comment pourrais-je rester là et la juger, agissant haut et fort ? Personne ne savait ce que l'avenir réservait.

Christiane a levé les yeux vers moi, son sourire tombant alors que nous nous arrêtions, mais je n'ai rien dit.

Reculant lentement, je la quittai et retournai dans la salle de bal, cherchant immédiatement Winter.

La musique grinçait dans mes oreilles et je l'ai vue parler à Michael et Emmy. J'ai marché pour elle.

Prenant sa main, je la vis sourire alors qu'elle reconnaissait instantanément ma sensation et m'attrapait avec ses deux mains.

« Où est Octavie ? » elle a demandé.

"Chasse au trésor avec Mads," marmonnai-je en l'attirant avec moi sans un mot ni un regard vers les deux autres. "Allez."

Sans aucun doute, elle s'est accrochée à moi alors que je la guidais dans le hall, sous le lustre aux chandelles et jusqu'à la porte des catacombes.

J'ai ouvert le loquet, l'ai fait entrer à l'intérieur et l'ai refermé derrière nous, la prenant immédiatement dans mes bras et descendant les escaliers.

"Qu'est-ce qui ne va pas?" demanda-t-elle en enroulant ses bras autour de mon cou.

"J'ai besoin de te tenir."

"Tu me tiens."

"Tu sais ce que je veux dire," dis-je en embrassant ses lèvres.

Elle n'a pas insisté davantage, me laissant juste la porter dans le bain et la remettre sur ses pieds. La lumière des bougies s'étendait jusque dans les catacombes, le jacuzzi déjà rempli d'eau et de vapeur s'élevant de la surface.

Je tendis la main, tournai le bouton, les becs du plafond s'animèrent et l'eau se déversa dans le petit bassin en un cercle d'une vingtaine de jets différents, presque comme une fontaine qui se déversait.

J'ai arraché ma veste et ma chemise, les laissant tomber au sol, suivis du reste de mes vêtements, puis je me suis mis au travail sur l'hiver. J'ai délacé le corset et baissé sa robe avant de retirer ses sous-vêtements, laissant les rubans dans ses cheveux.

La chaleur courut sous ma peau à sa vue, et je la pris dans mes bras, la soulevant. "Viens ici," haletai-je par-dessus ses lèvres.

Elle enroula ses jambes autour de moi et je grimpai dans l'immense baignoire, l'eau chaude envoyant des frissons dans tout mon corps.

Je m'assis, l'emmenant avec moi, la pluie tombant autour de nous alors que je la serrais contre moi et enfouis mon visage dans ses cheveux.

Elle se tendit, mais je serrai juste plus fort, essayant de me sentir à nouveau solide. Je détestais le doute, et la plupart du temps je m'occupais suffisamment pour ne pas m'inquiéter pour mes enfants, mais je ne savais pas plus que quiconque ce que je faisais. Je pouvais juger les gens qui m'ont élevé autant que je voulais, mais c'était moi qui serais jugé ensuite.

« Damon… » Murmura Winter, sachant que quelque chose n'allait pas.

"Je ne suis pas un bon père." Je poussai un soupir en la serrant contre moi. « Ivarsen n'a aucune discipline. Il ne sera pas entraîné. Fane est névrosé. Tout doit être parfait. Gunnar va nous faire exploser avec ses machines. Dag a refusé de manger un légume depuis sa naissance, et Octavia va se retrouver dans un putain d'asile quand elle découvrira que les vrais pirates ne sont que des terroristes avec des lance-grenades. Je déglutis, détestant qu'après des milliers d'années, il n'y ait toujours pas de méthode éprouvée pour élever des enfants. « Je ne sais pas quoi faire. Comment diable pourrais-je savoir ce qu'un bon parent fait et ne fait pas ? »

J'étais aussi ignorant que Christiane quand elle m'a eu. Kai avait raison. Ils avaient une meilleure chance de vivre avec plus de conseils. Je faisais tout de travers.

Les bras de Winter s'enroulèrent enfin autour de moi, et elle pressa ses lèvres contre ma tempe, ses seins contre mon corps.

« Un bon parent a des enfants heureux », m'a-t-elle chuchoté à l'oreille. "Nos enfants sont si heureux."

Elle embrassa ma joue puis mes lèvres, doucement et lentement. Je fermai les yeux, me délectant du bruit de l'eau et de sa sensation.

« Ils sont si heureux », me dit-elle encore. "Et tellement amoureux de toi."

85

Un flottement a frappé mon estomac, et j'ai souri un peu, incapable de le retenir.

Ils m'aiment, n'est-ce pas ?

"Et je suis tellement heureuse", a-t-elle ajouté.

Je reculai, la regardant alors que mes pensées recommençaient à se concentrer. Cela n'arrivait pas souvent, mais c'était difficile de ne pas me comparer. Les enfants de Kai avaient de bonnes manières et étaient assez calmes. Athos était intelligent, ambitieux et déterminé. Les enfants de Will ne l'ont jamais combattu sur quoi que ce soit. Ils ont fait ce qu'on leur avait dit la première fois qu'il a demandé.

Mes enfants...

Mais j'ai arrêté la pensée dans son élan, me souvenant qu'Ivar aidait sa mère à faire des pancakes ce matin.

Mes enfants pourraient être vraiment gentils, en fait, n'est-ce pas ?

Gunnar était si doué pour aider avec les déversements, pour que sa mère ne glisse pas. Fane l'a aidée à choisir des livres au magasin pour Dag et Octavia, décrivant les images et l'histoire, afin qu'elle sache quoi acheter.

C'étaient de bons enfants. J'inspirai et expirai, laissant tomber l'inquiétude pour le moment. Nous faisions du bon travail.

"Meilleur?" murmura-t-elle en embrassant ma mâchoire et en caressant mon cou.

Mes paupières se fermèrent et j'acquiesçai. "Ne t'arrête pas."

Elle se frotta contre moi, et je commençai à durcir, ma main caressant sa poitrine, mais ensuite un son aigu pénétra le plafond au-dessus de nos têtes, et nous nous arrêtâmes tous les deux, levant les yeux.

"C'était un cri ?" elle a demandé.

J'ai gémi. Et maintenant?

Sera

Je l'ai embrassée, ses lèvres rouges douces et chaudes alors que je caressais ses joues froides. Me reculant, je la regardai à travers le masque complexe en métal argenté qui couvrait son front, ses yeux me fixant à travers les fentes du dessin.

Se penchant, elle souffla par-dessus ma bouche et glissa rapidement une main dans mon pantalon, m'attrapant. « Vous pensez que votre femme soupçonne quelque chose ? taquina-t-elle.

J'ai haleté alors qu'elle me poingait, ne se souciant de rien en ce moment autre que de voir ses fesses nues, à l'exception de ce masque sur sa tête.

Je souris en mordillant sa lèvre inférieure. "On s'en fout?" me moquai-je. "Rien ne m'éloigne de toi."

Emmy a souri, plongeant sa bouche dans la mienne et retirant sa main de moi, afin qu'elle puisse enrouler ses bras autour de mon cou.

"Je t'aime tellement", m'a dit ma femme.
"Tu sais que c'est vrai?"

J'ai hoché la tête. "Mais vous pouvez toujours travailler dur pour le prouver."

"Je vais." Elle m'a encore embrassé. "Mais finis d'abord de danser avec moi."

Nous avons tourné, la musique dérivant à peine jusqu'au balcon du deuxième étage où nous avons dansé, le froid et la neige s'infiltrant jusqu'à nos os, mais elle souriait tellement que je n'étais pas sur le point d'arrêter ce qu'elle voulait.

Elle posa sa tête sur ma poitrine, me serrant contre elle.

J'ai adoré quand elle a fait ça. Tout le temps que j'ai passé à penser qu'elle n'avait pas besoin de moi, et maintenant je savais qu'elle en avait besoin.

Elle ne m'a pas retenu. Elle s'est accrochée à moi.

Nous avons regardé la forêt, la plupart des arbres sans feuilles, et la lanterne du clocher visible à travers les branches.

"Où est sa tombe?" Emmy a demandé.

Je n'avais pas besoin de lui demander de qui elle parlait, la flamme éternelle de Reverie Cross scintillant dans le clocher au loin.

C'était étrange qu'elle ait attendu si longtemps pour poser cette question, mais ce n'était pas un étranger que personne d'autre n'avait jamais eu.

Comme je n'ai pas répondu, elle a demandé : « Votre grand-père l'aimait-il ?

Je resserrai mes bras autour d'elle. "Je ne lui ai jamais demandé."

C'était un sujet dont j'étais éternellement curieux, mais je ne pourrais jamais l'aborder avec lui. Peut-être que je serais déçu si les réponses étaient plus ennuyeuses que mon imagination.

Peut-être que j'avais peur que les réponses changent la façon dont je l'aimais.

« L'a-
t-il
tuée ?
murm
ura
Emmy
."Je
ne lui
dema
nderai
pas."

Jamai

s.

"Il pourrait être le seul à savoir ce qui s'est passé cette nuit-là", a-t-elle insisté.

*Je sais.*Et il ne vivrait pas beaucoup plus longtemps pour raconter l'histoire.

« Personne ne sait où se trouve sa tombe, alors ? » demanda-t-elle à nouveau.

« Nulle part près d'Edward, » lui dis-je. "C'est tout ce que je sais."

Je la blottis contre moi, voulant profiter au maximum du temps qu'il nous restait avant que les enfants ne rentrent à la maison, et discuter de Reverie Cross n'était pas ce que j'avais en tête.

"Alors, tu m'aimes ?" J'ai taquiné.

"Je suis presque sûr que je vous ai dit que je l'ai fait il y a à peine trente-neuf secondes." je me suis moqué. J'aimais l'entendre plus fréquemment. Elle le savait.

Elle rit, pressant sa bouche contre la mienne. "Je vous aime."

Je me suis déplacé sur ses lèvres, gelant mon cul ici, mais la promesse chaleureuse de son corps m'a rendu dur et prêt.

« Je veux aller quelque part », lui ai-je dit.

Catacombes, garde-manger, chambre d'amis... n'importe où.

"Je veux danser un peu plus", gémit-elle.

J'arquai un sourcil. « Et si tu dansais pour moi ?

Je pourrais vivre avec ça.

Un sourire malicieux traversa ses lèvres et elle se mordit la lèvre inférieure. "Faites la course."

Et avant que je puisse répondre, elle s'est éloignée, a remonté sa robe et s'est mise à courir.

Un rire a grondé en moi, la regardant rentrer dans la maison avec ses talons hauts avant que je ne sprinte, la pourchassant.

Se précipitant dans le salon, elle a crié alors que je la suivais et nous avons tous les deux couru dans le couloir, vers les chambres d'amis.

Mais ensuite, elle s'est arrêtée tout d'un coup et a crié, son dos se raidissant.

"Sera!" elle a pleuré.

Mon sourire est tombé, et je me suis précipité à ses côtés, la saisissant.

« Quoi ? »

Mais ensuite j'ai baissé les yeux et j'ai vu une mare sanglante sur le parquet, un corps allongé dans le couloir.

Je pris une inspiration et la tirai en arrière. « Qu'est-ce que c'est que ce bordel ? » "Oh mon Dieu." Elle couvrit sa bouche avec sa main.

"Que se passe-t-il?" Kai a appelé d'en bas et j'ai regardé par-dessus la balustrade pour le voir debout dans le hall.

"Se dépêcher!" Je lui ai fait signe.

A genoux, j'ai essayé de distinguer le visage du type dans le noir, mais il était face contre terre, seul le côté gauche était visible.

Qui…? Que diable s'est-il passé ?

"Bébé, allume les lumières", lui ai-je dit.

J'ai pressé mes doigts, trouvant son cou pour vérifier son pouls, mais je n'ai pas pu en trouver un. La lumière éclaira finalement le couloir alors que des pas frappaient les escaliers, tout le monde courant après nous.

"Que diable?" dit Kai en s'arrêtant à côté du corps. "Qui est-ce?" Comment pourrais-je savoir?

"Est-il mort?" J'ai entendu Michael demander.

Aucune idée. Je le fixai, un jeune homme blond en tenue de ville, du sang coulant de sa tête. Je ne l'ai pas reconnu et il n'était pas habillé pour la fête.

"Qui est-ce?" demanda Rika.

J'ai secoué ma tête.

Quelqu'un nous dépassa en courant pendant que je fouillais ses poches pour trouver une pièce d'identité, mais quand j'ai tendu la main sous sa veste, je l'ai senti.

J'hésitai, le pouls palpitant dans mon cou. *Merde.*

Je l'ai retourné, j'ai creusé sous son bras et j'ai sorti le pistolet de son étui. Il reposait dans ma paume, la réalisation commençant à nous frapper tous au même moment. Les seules personnes qui avaient des armes étaient Lev et David, et ce n'était ni l'un ni l'autre.

"Les enfants sont partis !" cria une femme.

*Quoi?*J'ai bondi sur mes pieds alors que tout le monde se retournait pour croiser le regard de Mme Cuthbert.

"Quels enfants ?" j'ai aboyé. "Ils sont au théâtre." Et puis j'ai pointé du menton vers Emmy, lui lançant mon téléphone. "Appelez Mlle Englestat." Elle avait le enfants au théâtre. "Faites-lui faire un décompte."

Elle hocha la tête, ses mains tremblant alors qu'elle composait le numéro.

"Mads et Octavia," murmura Damon, ses yeux inquiets rencontrant les miens. "Ils sont restés derrière."

Mads et Octavia… J'ai jeté les yeux sur la nounou.

« Ils ne sont pas dans leurs chambres », cria-t-elle.

Et mon visage s'est décomposé, réalisant que c'étaient les enfants dont elle parlait.

Tout le monde a couru.

« Tavi ! » Banks a couru dans le couloir jusqu'aux chambres que les enfants utilisaient quand ils étaient ici.

"Folle !" Kai se précipita dans l'autre couloir où il bifurqua pour fouiller la galerie où son fils aimait se cacher.

"Folle !" plus de voix ont appelé alors que tout le monde se déployait.

Ma bouche est devenue sèche. J'ai redescendu, cherchant le pouls du mec et ne le trouvant pas. Mettant mes doigts sous son nez, j'attendis de sentir la chaleur de son souffle.

Il n'y avait rien.

95

D'autres bruits de pas montèrent les escaliers, et je me levai à nouveau, rassemblant les possibilités dans ma tête.

« Il est mort », dis-je.

« Ce n'était pas nous », dis-je à la tête de Lev, et je levai les yeux pour le voir, lui et David, debout en haut des escaliers, essoufflés. "Nous n'avons rien vu." "Cela est évident!" Les banques ont grogné.

« La porte s'ouvre toutes les dix secondes avec des invités, Banks ! cria Lev. "N'importe qui aurait pu entrer. Je t'ai dit que nous avions besoin de plus de sécurité."

"Mais vous ne vouliez pas tous" des gardes armés et un détecteur de métaux à la porte d'entrée "", a ajouté David, citant Michael.

Michael attrapa son col, le repoussant. « Fouillez la maison. Aller!" Damon, Banks et Michael ont couru dans et hors des chambres, cherchant à nouveau. "Des fous !" ils ont appelé. « Octavie !

Je glissai le pistolet dans le dos de mon pantalon et fis signe à Kai. "Prends ses pieds."

"Nous avons besoin de la police", a expliqué Emmy. "Ne le bougez pas."

96

« Nous n'appelons personne tant que nous n'avons pas trouvé les enfants », grinça Kai.

Nous ne savions pas comment cela s'était passé. Nous devions le savoir avant d'impliquer les flics.

« Octavie ! Damon a beuglé, et j'ai juré que je pouvais entendre sa respiration frénétique d'ici.

"Attendez, les caméras..." éclata Rika.

Se retournant, elle courut à son bureau, son ordinateur configuré pour accéder aux caméras de rue et à la sécurité de la maison. Elle avait une vue sur presque chaque centimètre carré de la ville.

Kai et moi avons jeté le corps dans sa chambre et celle de Michael, avons fermé la porte, renversé le tapis dans le couloir pour couvrir le sang et couru après tout le monde, chargeant dans son bureau.

"Retourne", j'ai entendu Michael lui dire.

En appuyant sur des boutons et en tournant un bouton, elle a rembobiné les images, rejouant les événements de la nuit. Il n'y avait pas de caméras à l'intérieur de la maison, mais elles couvraient l'extérieur et le terrain. J'ai deviné que cela changerait après

97

ce soir. Michael aurait la compagnie ici le matin, ajoutant une sécurité supplémentaire.

Elle s'arrêta, voyant Mads et Octavia se précipiter par la porte latérale de la cuisine, courant frénétiquement comme si elles essayaient de s'échapper, mais...

Une voiture attendait. Mon cœur s'est logé dans ma gorge. Deux hommes ont sauté, et avant que les enfants ne sachent ce qui se passait, ils ont été jetés à l'intérieur et la voiture est partie en courant.

"Non," haleta Damon.

"Qu'est-ce que c'est?" L'hiver a pleuré.

Il la tenait juste contre lui.

"Attendez, attendez, qui est-ce?" Kai désigna le blond assis sur le siège passager. "Agrandir!"

Rika a rembobiné à nouveau, l'a rattrapé alors qu'il sortait de la voiture pour aider à emmener les enfants et a mis la vidéo en pause, améliorant la prise de vue.

Banks gémit. "Ilia Oblonsky."

La colonne vertébrale de Kai se redressa et il respira fort. Ilia était un employé de Gabriel Torrance il y a des années. Les banques l'ont fait expulser du pays lorsqu'elle a hérité de la succession de son père.

"Et qui-est-ce?" Michael loucha vers l'autre qui était sorti du SUV.

"Je ne peux pas dire," répondit Rika.

Mais j'ai fixé la tête brune que je connaissais n'importe où, parce que je le connaissais bien.

Mon Dieu.

— Taylor Dinescu, murmurai-je.

Tout le monde s'est tourné vers moi, mon passage à Blackchurch dressant toujours sa vilaine tête.

"Jésus, merde," marmonna Damon. "Comment se sont-ils trouvés ?"

Je n'en avais aucune idée. Peut-être qu'il y avait un groupe Facebook pour les gens qui nous détestaient. Un sentiment de naufrage m'a frappé, parce que je savais. Je le savais il y a des années. C'était un déséquilibré que j'avais ignoré, et je n'aurais pas dû.

Mais ensuite, Banks s'est retourné. « Kai ? »

Je suivis son regard, voyant Kai sortir de la pièce, la rage dans les yeux.

« C'est mon tour », lui dit-il. « Je t'ai laissé t'occuper de lui la dernière fois. Pas cette fois."

Mais avant que j'aie pu comprendre ce qu'il voulait dire, il s'est échappé de la pièce, et cela n'a pas pris de temps du tout avant que nous courions tous après lui.

Le bal continuait toujours en bas, mais au lieu de dégager les lieux ou de trouver des excuses à nos invités, nous n'avons pas perdu une minute de plus.

"Donnez-moi votre téléphone", a dit Rika à Banks.

Sans aucun doute, elle le lui tendit alors que nous dévalions les escaliers. Des larmes ont coulé sur les joues de Banks, mais elle n'a pas fait de bruit autrement.

« Je te connecte aux caméras de la rue », lui dit Rika en tapotant sur son portable. «Ils ont franchi la porte il y a environ quatre-vingt-dix secondes, probablement en direction de la ville, mais gardez un œil sur eux et assurez-vous. Nous suivrons.

Banks hocha la tête, Rika lui rendit son téléphone et tout le monde se précipita par la porte d'entrée, attrapant les clés des voitures sur le chemin.

Mais j'ai aperçu quelque chose et je me suis arrêté.

Ils ont tous viré autour de moi, vidant le hall, mais j'ai fixé l'horloge grand-père, son pendule figé et l'aiguille des minutes s'est arrêtée sur dix heures neuf minutes.

Tenant mon poignet, j'ai vérifié ma montre, voyant qu'il était en fait vingt-trois heures après l'heure.

Je jetai à nouveau un coup d'œil à l'horloge.

"Qu'est-ce que c'est?" Emmy se précipita vers moi.

"L'horloge s'est arrêtée." Je ne pouvais pas respirer. "Dix-oh-neuf. C'est alors que Reverie Cross est mort.

Je veux dire, je ne croyais pas vraiment à cette merde, mais je savais aussi que Madden était le seul à avoir refusé d'allumer une bougie sur EverNight. Un peu bizarre.

Elle m'a entraînée, nous avons tous les deux couru vers les portes arrière de l'un des SUV, Kai et Banks s'empilant à l'avant. Michael et Damon montèrent dans l'autre voiture avec Winter et Rika, et Kai glissa la clé dedans, s'arrêtant soudainement.

Il a tapoté sur l'horloge numérique, et j'ai zoné, voyant aussi dix oh-neuf sur l'horloge de la voiture.

"Que diable?" Kaï grogna.

Mais il n'arrêtait pas de s'inquiéter. « À quelle distance de nous sont-ils ? » demanda-t-il à sa femme.

"Je viens d'arriver au village", lui dit-elle en regardant son écran. "Se dépêcher."

Nous nous sommes attachés et j'ai lancé un regard inquiet à Emmy à côté de moi.

"Ce n'est pas EverNight," murmura-t-elle.

"Ce n'est pas obligé."

Reverie Cross avait toute l'année pour frapper, et bien que je sache qu'une flamme allumée le lendemain matin signifiait que vous étiez en sécurité, je n'avais jamais pensé à ce qui arrivait à ceux qui n'allumaient pas du tout de bougie.

"Allons-y!" J'ai appelé.

Kai s'est élancé, accélérant les gaz, et nous avons couru dans l'allée, les phares de Michael brillant sur notre queue.

Kai a chargé sur la route, les pneus tournant sous nous sur le bitume enneigé. Passant à la vitesse inférieure, il descendit la rue à toute allure, passa devant les autres maisons illuminées de feux de joie, de lanternes et de lumières de Noël.

« Êtes-vous arrivé à Engelstat ? Je me tournai vers Emmy, me souvenant de ce que je lui avais demandé de faire.

"Oui, les enfants sont en sécurité." Elle acquiesça. «Les banques ont envoyé la sécurité au théâtre.

102

Ils resteront là jusqu'à notre arrivée. J'ai hoché la tête une fois. Bien.

Au contraire, ils étaient probablement plus en sécurité là-bas. Des tonnes de gens, tout l'endroit enfermé...

"Où sont-ils maintenant?" J'ai demandé à Banks.

Elle hésita, étudiant son écran et changeant de point de vue. "En route vers Old Pointe Road," répondit-elle finalement, puis regarda Kai. « Ils n'iraient pas à la station, n'est-ce pas ? Meridian City, peut-être ?

Il secoua la tête, tournant les yeux à gauche et à droite alors qu'il courait à ce qui ressemblait à une centaine de miles à l'heure. "Gardez juste vos yeux sur eux."

Je regardai par la fenêtre, serrant ma mâchoire si fort que ça me faisait mal. Taylor Dinescu. Nous n'avions pas joué avec Blackchurch pour lui depuis la dernière fois que nous l'avions vu ce soir-là au Cove. Nous avons tout jeté sur lui et sa famille, l'envoyant en prison, parce qu'il méritait d'être là. Non seulement pour ce qui l'a fait envoyer à Blackchurch, mais aussi pour des raisons personnelles.

Il avait blessé Emmy. Beaucoup. Et il a adoré le faire.

Et quand il a finalement réussi à s'en sortir il y a six ans, j'ai embauché quelqu'un pour garder un œil sur lui pendant un certain temps – s'assurer qu'il n'avait pas d'idées – mais je savais qu'il ne méritait pas une seconde chance. On aurait dû le renvoyer.

Ou traité avec lui de façon permanente. C'était lui qui avait l'argent. Pas Ilia. Si je m'en étais occupé, nous ne serions pas là.

"Ça aurait pu être nos enfants," marmonnai-je, les larmes aux yeux.

"Ce sont nos enfants", a répondu Em.

Je la regardai alors qu'elle tendait la main et me prenait la main. Je ne pouvais pas imaginer ce que Damon ressentait en ce moment.

Je n'en saurais pas vraiment la pleine mesure tant que ce n'était pas l'un des miens.

« Que s'est-il passé dans cette pièce ? Banks a demandé à Kai. "Quelque chose a mal tourné s'ils ont laissé un cadavre derrière eux. Comment n'avons-nous rien entendu ni rien vu ?

"Nous allons les trouver", a déclaré Kai. "Mads est intelligent."

« Il se serait battu », lui dit Banks en pleurant à nouveau. «Ils auraient dû lui faire du mal pour le faire monter dans cette voiture. Avez-vous vu sur la caméra s'ils l'ont frappé ou non ? »

Il secoua la tête mais ne répondit pas.

Mes yeux brûlaient en voyant Banks si effrayé pour la première fois. J'ai tourné la tête par la fenêtre. Ce serait notre fin. S'il arrivait quelque chose à ces enfants...

Nous avions des minutes. Quelques minutes avant qu'ils ne disparaissent pour toujours.

« Regarde-moi », lui dit Kai, essayant également de garder les yeux sur la route. "Pas aujourd'hui."

Banks hocha la tête mais semblait toujours sur le point de craquer.

J'ai entendu une ceinture de sécurité se détacher, et Emmy était soudainement sur mes genoux, forçant mon visage à se retourner et mes yeux sur elle.

Je les ai fermés, cependant. Je leur avais apporté ça. Et si pire arrivait un jour à nos enfants ? Dans quelle vie l'ai-je amenée ?

"Regardez-moi." Elle m'a secoué.

J'ai ouvert les yeux.

"Nous ne pourrions pas être quelqu'un d'autre", a-t-elle déclaré. "Ce n'est pas ta faute."

J'ai levé les yeux vers elle, tous les doutes et inquiétudes que j'avais l'habitude de cacher étaient mis à nu pour elle, parce qu'elle savait toujours ce que je pensais. Elle pouvait me lire aussi bien qu'elle-même.

Je ne voulais être personne d'autre. Mais je ne voulais pas non plus que les enfants subissent les conséquences de nos choix.

J'enroulai mes bras autour d'elle et la regardai dans les yeux. "Je t'aime," murmurai-je. "Merci pour mes enfants."

Si je n'avais pas l'occasion de le redire...

Son sourire se dessina. "Idem."

Je me suis accrochée à elle, son odeur et ses yeux me rappelant nos enfants et tout ce que j'aimais dans le fait de me réveiller chaque jour.

Nous avions le droit d'être ici, et nous ne l'avons pas demandé.

Me penchant vers le bas, j'ai serré les deux côtés de la fente de sa robe et l'ai déchirée jusqu'à sa cuisse, donnant à ses jambes de la place pour bouger. "Allons chercher ces enfoirés."

Elle m'a embrassé alors que Kai fonçait dans le village, mais a immédiatement freiné.

"Que diable?" aboya-t-il.

Je m'éloignai d'Em, louchant par le pare-brise avant pour voir la rue bondée de monde, malgré les flocons épais et blancs qui tombaient. J'ai jeté un coup d'œil au théâtre, remarquant les deux hommes de Banks juste à l'intérieur des portes, gardant les enfants.

J'ai expiré, regardant les costumes, les masques et les foyers qui brillaient autour du village alors que la musique jouait et que les gens souriaient.

Le Père Noël s'est assis dans le gazebo, une file d'une douzaine d'enfants attendant de le rencontrer.

« La chasse au trésor », lui ai-je rappelé. C'est pourquoi tout le monde était sorti. Nous n'aurions pas pu mieux planifier cet enlèvement pour Taylor et Ilia. Des tonnes d'activités pour se perdre.

Je regardai derrière moi, ne voyant pas les autres. Michael a dû parcourir un long chemin, sachant à quoi ressemblerait le village.

"Passez devant la cathédrale", lui a dit Emmy. "Prenez la voie jusqu'à Old Pointe."

Il a klaxonné et allumé ses phares alors que les gens prenaient leur temps pour s'écarter du putain de chemin. Lentement, la rue enneigée s'éclaircit.

« Kai, vas-y ! Banks a crié.

Il fit une embardée, passa devant le belvédère, Sticks et la White Crow Tavern, donnant un coup de volant et dérapant au coin de la rue.

Banks gémit, tenant la barre de sécurité au-dessus de sa fenêtre, et je pouvais dire qu'elle perdait la tête. Plus ces enfants n'étaient pas dans nos bras, plus nous avions de chances de ne jamais les retrouver.

Je n'avais aucune idée de ce que Taylor et Ilia planifiaient, mais s'ils avaient voulu leur mort, ils l'auraient fait à la maison. Il n'y avait aucun moyen qu'ils prévoyaient de les rendre, cependant. Ce serait suicidaire.

Des pensées de choses bien pires ont envahi ma tête et mon estomac s'est retourné, sachant ce qui était arrivé aux enfants du monde entier. L'horreur qui pourrait nous attendre si nous les perdions ce soir.

Je me suis frotté les yeux, la sueur sur mon front recouvrant ma main.

Les phares ont creusé un trou dans l'obscurité devant moi, des flocons de neige flottant au sol alors que le pistolet s'enfonçait dans mon dos. J'ai été tenté de l'utiliser.

Dieu, j'ai été tenté d'amener notre famille sur cette ligne ce soir.

"Arrêt!" Banks a crié. Elle a pointé devant et tout le monde a regardé, voyant des feux arrière dans le fossé au bord de la route. Mon cœur martelait dans ma poitrine alors que Kai se hissait derrière le SUV et s'arrêtait, tout le monde sachant sans un mot que c'était la même voiture.

Que diable s'est-il passé ? Les enfants...

Nous avons sauté de la voiture, le froid nous mordillant le visage alors que nous courions vers le SUV noir accidenté.

Le soulagement et la peur m'envahirent en même temps.

Taylor était effondré, la tête au-dessus du volant, la vitre partiellement baissée, et j'ai bondi dans le ravin en m'agrippant à la poignée de la portière.

« Espèce de fils de pute ! criai-je en me penchant par-dessus la fenêtre et en essayant de l'attraper. Il a chancelé, le visage ensanglanté, mais la putain de voiture s'est écrasée entre deux arbres et je n'ai pas pu ouvrir la porte. « Octavie ! Emmy a crié.

Suivi par les banques. "Des fous !"

Je me précipitai vers l'arrière de la voiture et ouvris le hayon, rampant sur la banquette arrière jusqu'à l'enfoiré.

"Ils ne sont pas là !" cria Banks en rampant derrière moi.

Emmy a cassé la vitre côté conducteur juste au moment où j'atteignais Taylor. Il se retourna, sortant une arme à feu, mais juste à ce moment-là, elle tira sa main, faisant tomber l'arme au sol, et fouetta la crête de sa paume directement dans son cou, lui écrasant la gorge.

Il h. Kai lui a-t-il appris cela ? Semblait familier.

Le sang a emmêlé les cheveux de Taylor et coulé sur son visage. Je l'ai attrapé, agrippant sa mâchoire. "Où sont-elles?" beuglai-je. "Qu'est-ce que tu as fait?"

Mais juste à ce moment-là, je l'ai vu. Mon estomac se retourna et je grimaçai, détournant les yeux un instant. Jésus putain de Christ. Qu'est-ce que c'est ?

Son putain de globe oculaire pendait juste à l'extérieur de son orbite, du sang coulant également de l'autre. Comment est-ce arrivé?

« Ça... ça... » haleta-t-il, essayant de faire sortir les mots. « Ce gamin est fou. Il a tué Gibbons.

Hein? "Qui?" j'ai aboyé.

Tu sais quoi, je m'en fiche."Où sont-elles?" Je poings son col, le secouant.

Et où était Ilia ?

Emmy s'écarta, laissant entrer Kai, le père de Mads agrippant Taylor avec moi, nous lui serrant tous les deux le crâne.

J'ai placé mon pouce juste entre son nez et son œil, prêt à creuser. "Maintenant, ou je prends l'autre !"

Il ferma la bouche, et j'eus à peine le temps de réaliser ce qu'il faisait avant qu'il me crache au visage.

Kai grogna, l'attrapa et enfouit son pouce dans ses yeux, menaçant de l'aveugler complètement.

« Ahh ! » il a crié.

"Où?" a crié Kaï.

"Le port de plaisance !" il pleure. "Le port de plaisance !"

Je me précipitai hors de la voiture, attrapant la main d'Emmy alors que nous nous précipitions tous vers notre SUV. Lev et

111

David se sont arrêtés, sortant de leur voiture, après avoir probablement suivi le téléphone de Banks.

"Le pape", leur a dit Kai, mais il a ensuite tendu la main vers Taylor et a sorti un masque blanc.

Ce n'était pas l'un des nôtres. Plus comme un masque fantôme complet. L'a-t-il reconnu ?

Ou…

Mon estomac s'est noué. Ils étaient à la fête.

Jésus Christ.

Kai jeta le masque dans la voiture, puis se dirigea vers la nôtre, ouvrant sa portière d'un coup sec. « Le douzième étage », ordonna-t-il.

"Oui, monsieur," répondit David.

*Bonne idée.*Nous ne confiions Taylor aux soins de personne cette fois. Nous avions un endroit pour le cacher. S'il a survécu.

Ils ont couru chercher Taylor alors que Banks sautait sur son téléphone. "La marina," dit-elle à quelqu'un, probablement Damon. "Tuez-le si vous devez." Et s'il vous plaît dépêchez-vous.

J'ouvris la porte arrière, laissant entrer Emmy en premier.

"C'était un bon coup, bébé," lui dis-je, me souvenant de son petit tour de main sur sa gorge. "John Wick, n'est-ce pas?"

"John Wick 2."

J'ai hoché la tête, me précipitant après elle. "Oh, d'accord."

Michael

"Je te tiendrai au courant", a dit Rika à sa mère au téléphone. "Ne vous inquiétez pas." Elle a écouté, puis a hoché la tête en me regardant. "Dès que nous savons quelque chose, oui."

Elle raccrocha et me tendit le téléphone. Je l'ai mis dans ma poche, Damon sur le siège du conducteur devant moi et Winter se tordant les mains à côté de lui.

J'ai entendu un bip de notification, puis Damon a appuyé sur l'écran de son portable.

"Qu'est-ce que c'est?" demanda Rika.

"Banks a envoyé un texto", nous a-t-il dit. "Les enfants sont à la marina." "Est-ce que Banks les a?" ai-je lâché.

Mais il a secoué la tête, appuyant sur le gaz, le moteur tournant sous nous. "Je ne pense pas."

« Damon… » supplia Winter, et je pus voir ses genoux trembler.

Il lui serra la main. "Ils ne feront rien."

"Ils ne prévoient peut-être pas de le faire, mais je doute que ce cadavre à l'étage ait été prévu non plus", a-t-elle souligné. "Quelque chose s'est mal passé. Ils auront plus peur maintenant.

Rika s'avança et posa sa main sur le bras de Winter.

"S'ils allaient…" J'ai commencé, mais j'ai pensé qu'il valait mieux le dire à voix haute. « Ils l'auraient fait à la maison. Ils veulent une rançon ou quelque chose comme ça.

Winter s'arrêta un moment, baissant la tête. « Ou ils les vendent », marmonna-t-elle. "Ou les apporter à quelqu'un d'autre."

Jésus. Je fermai les yeux en gémissant. Nous connaissions tous les pires scénarios, et aucun d'entre eux ne se terminait heureusement pour nous si nous ne rattrapions pas ces enfants dans les dix prochaines minutes.

Je détestais qu'elle laisse ces pensées s'envenimer, mais… ça nous a gardés alertes, je suppose.

"Allez-y," aboya Rika. « Faites le tour de lui.

Damon fit une embardée dans la mauvaise voie, dépassa une autre voiture, puis donna un nouveau coup de volant, accélérant devant elle.

Reprenant mon téléphone, j'appelai Athos.

J'aurais dû l'appeler tout de suite. Merde.

"Hé," gloussa-t-elle, et je pouvais entendre le bavardage de ses amis en arrière-plan. « Je ne bois pas. Je pourrais faire des bisous. Et je soulève un peu l'enfer. Fier de moi?"

"Allez au théâtre", ai-je lâché. "À présent. C'est une urgence. Reste là jusqu'à ce que je vienne te chercher.

Il y eut un silence, et je m'attendais à moitié à être interrogé, mais elle ne se débattit pas.

Je l'ai entendue déglutir. "D'accord," répondit-elle calmement. "J'enverrai un texto quand je serai là-bas."

"Je t'aime," dis-je.

"Je t'aime aussi."

Nous avons raccroché et j'ai regardé Rika qui écoutait, ses épaules se détendant lorsque j'ai hoché la tête.

Nous n'avons jamais réagi de manière excessive, et Athos le savait. Si j'avais l'air inquiet, j'avais raison, et elle devait faire ce qu'on lui disait.

116

Rika tendit la main derrière et ramassa une veste de la troisième rangée, l'enfila, puis creusa sous le siège, en sortant une lame. Elle les a gardés dans toutes nos voitures et à divers endroits de la maison pour un accès immédiat.

Mais je posai ma main sur la sienne, l'arrêtant.

Elle croisa mon regard et je secouai la tête. Non pas cette fois.

Ses yeux se rétrécirent, confus. "Tu ne peux pas être sérieux," murmura-t-elle. "Je suis toujours avec toi."

Mon cœur me faisait mal, parce que je n'avais jamais voulu faire quoi que ce soit sans elle. Elle était la raison pour laquelle nous étions qui nous étions. Tout avait commencé avec elle.

Mes yeux tombèrent sur son ventre, notre fils commençant à se montrer de plus en plus chaque jour.

"J'ai besoin que tu sois avec lui," lui dis-je.

À tout prix.

"Mais Octavia et Madden..."

"Nous les aurons."

Bien sûr, elle était nécessaire. Et toujours voulu.

117

J'ai touché son visage, levant son menton vers moi, et le regard dans ses yeux m'a ramené à cette nuit où elle avait treize ans, criant après moi par-dessus le capot de ma voiture. « J'ai attendu trop longtemps pour nous voir toi et moi nous promener en une seule personne, » murmurai-je.

Nous aimions Athos et nous avons eu de la chance, car je me foutais de la mère qui l'avait laissée chez la baby-sitter à sept ans et qui n'était jamais revenue, ni du père qu'elle n'avait jamais connu.

Elle était faite pour nous.

Mais je mourais d'envie d'avoir une autre chance d'être papa.

Damon se précipita sur le parking de la marina, des falaises des deux côtés et de la neige blanche tombant sur la mer. Rika hocha finalement la tête, sachant que c'était aussi loin qu'elle allait.

"Je vais appeler Recherche et sauvetage." Elle m'a ôté mon téléphone des mains. "Et dirigez la police quand ils arrivent ici."

Je pris son visage et me penchai, l'embrassant alors que Damon et Winter sautaient hors de la voiture, et que des phares nous tombaient dessus par derrière.

Kai et Will étaient là.

« Verrouillez les portes », murmurai-je contre sa bouche.

"Aller." Elle m'embrassa à nouveau, ses joues mouillées de larmes. "Se dépêcher. Rapporte les."

J'ai sauté de la voiture, des flocons de glace frappant mon visage alors que je clignais des yeux contre la chute de neige.

"Allons-y!" a crié Kaï.

J'ai couru, regardant une fois de plus Rika à travers le pare-brise, mais elle était déjà au téléphone alors qu'elle se penchait sur les sièges avant, frappant les serrures.

Nous avons dévalé les marches et sur le quai, à la recherche de tout signe de mouvement ou de vie parmi les bateaux, ou en mer.

"Mon Dieu, ça va mal", a déclaré Emmy, tirant le manteau de Will autour d'elle alors qu'elle clignait des yeux contre l'averse.

L'océan noir se profilait au-delà, les ténèbres engloutissant toute lumière. Dieu, il n'y avait rien. Pas de coup de pied dans le sillage d'un bateau. Pas de lumières. Où étaient-ils?

J'ai attrapé mon téléphone, mais ma poche était vide. J'avais oublié que Rika l'avait. Nous avions besoin de plus d'yeux sur la ville. Je ne savais pas d'où Kai tenait ses informations, mais elles pouvaient être n'importe où sauf ici.

"M. Mori !" quelqu'un a appelé.

Nous nous sommes tous retournés et mes yeux ont finalement aperçu le vieil homme sur le balcon du deuxième étage du bureau de la marina.

Doones avait environ soixante-cinq ans et le dernier loup de mer de Thunder Bay pouvait se vanter de l'époque où nous étions fiers de notre chaudrée de palourdes plutôt que de nos dégustations de fromage et de vin.

Kai se précipita en criant : « Avez-vous vu Octavia et Madden ce soir ?

Par où sont-ils allés ?

"Je n'ai rien vu", cria-t-il, de la vapeur s'échappant de sa bouche alors que des cheveux gris filandreux sortaient de sous son bonnet d'hiver. "C'est une tempête hivernale qui arrive !" Il tendit la main, l'annonçant comme si nous étions tous aveugles. "Juste quelques gars plus tôt sont venus de Pithom sur un hors-bord."

J'ai fait un pas en avant. "Quoi?" Pithom ? Ils sont venus de mon yacht ?

« Pithom est amarré dans les
Keys pour l'hiver. Ce n'est pas
ici!" "Non, ça flotte à environ
un mile," m'informa-t-il,
"mais..." Il se pencha d'un
côté à l'autre comme s'il
cherchait derrière nous.

"Eh bien, leur hors-bord est parti maintenant, alors ils ont dû revenir et y retourner."

Et il ne vit pas quand ils étaient revenus. Ce qui signifiait que les enfants auraient pu être avec eux.

Je tournai les yeux vers Damon. « Tu as la clé ? »

Il fouilla dans la poche de son pantalon et en sortit son trousseau de clés, celui en argent avec la poignée noire immédiatement visible. Il avait emmené le hors-bord de la compagnie la semaine dernière, essayant de faire passer un drone au-dessus de Deadlow Island, mais c'était juste entre nous. Rika et Kai auraient nos fesses s'ils savaient qu'on espionnait les Moreau.

"Aller!" Damon nous a tous commandés.

Nous avons tous couru le long du quai, le bateau de course rouge flottant à sa place habituelle et Doones criant derrière nous.

121

"Monsieur, non !" il pleure. « La visibilité se détériore de minute en minute. Nous pouvons appeler les garde-côtes. "Pas le temps!" beugla Kai.

"Putain," dit Damon.

"Est, par le sud-est", a crié Doones, "à en juger d'où ils venaient quand ils sont arrivés il y a quelques heures !"

Kai lui fit un signe de remerciement.

"Je le jure, Kai," grogna Will. "Tu dis à ce gamin d'allumer une putain de bougie à partir de maintenant."

« Tais-toi », lui dit Kai.

Tout le monde embarqua sur le bateau, Em, Winter et Banks s'installèrent sur la banquette arrière tandis que Kai démarrait le moteur. Damon était assis à côté de lui et Will se tenait au milieu.

J'ai posé un pied sur l'engin mais je me suis arrêté. Jetant un coup d'œil par-dessus mon épaule, j'ai vu les SUV sur le parking, Rika cachée derrière les vitres teintées.

Cela n'a pris qu'un moment, mais j'ai roulé des yeux et soupiré. "Attends," grinçai-je.

Je ne pouvais pas la quitter.

Remontant le quai, j'ai bondi les marches, l'air froid traversant mes poumons.

"Michael!" cria Kai.

J'entendis la serrure de la porte cliquer un instant avant de tirer sur la poignée pour l'ouvrir.

Rika fronça les sourcils en me regardant bouche bée.

Mais je n'ai pas eu le temps de m'expliquer. Attrapant sa main, je l'ai tirée hors de la voiture, nous nous sommes tous les deux lancés aussi vite que possible dans ses talons. Je ne voulais pas qu'elle tombe, et certainement pas avant les prochains mois.

Nous avons couru le long du quai, et je l'ai tirée à bord, la poussant dans un siège et resserrant ma veste sur celle qu'elle portait déjà.

« Tu restes assise », lui ai-je dit.

Elle acquiesça.

"Aller aller!" cria Damon après Kai.

Kai appuya sur les gaz, les hélices soulevant de l'eau derrière nous, et je m'agrippai au dossier de la chaise de Damon, me tenant alors que nous nous éloignions du port.

Le vent glacial frappa mes cheveux, gelant ma bouche, mais je me précipitai devant nous, à la recherche du moindre signe des enfants ou de l'autre bateau.

Comment ont-ils obtenu Pithom ? Pourquoi?

Ils ont dû prévoir de les cacher en mer indéfiniment. Sinon, pourquoi auraient-ils eu besoin d'un si grand navire ?

Le vent a tranché ma peau alors que des pensées tourbillonnaient dans ma tête.

Ilia avait été plusieurs fois sur Pithom au cours de son travail avec le père de Damon, et Gabriel avait été plusieurs fois sur le yacht avec le mien.

Il aurait connu le bateau. J'en aurais su assez sur nous pour y avoir probablement accès.

Je savais que j'aurais dû vendre cet enfoiré. Il s'était passé trop de conneries dessus, mais au lieu de m'en débarrasser, je l'avais envoyé dans le sud pour la saison afin qu'il soit réaménagé.

Nom de Dieu.

« Que diable s'est-il passé à la maison ? J'ai entendu Emmy demander. « Et dans la voiture ? Son œil a été arraché ?

J'ai tourné la tête. « L'œil de qui ? »

Mais c'est Banks qui a répondu. "La voiture que nous avons vue sur la caméra. Il a été écrasé près de Old Pointe. Dinescu était en mauvais état », a-t-elle ajouté.

124

"Mais cela laisse juste Ilia", a crié Will par-dessus le vent. "Il ne pourrait pas porter Tavi et Mads."

"S'il avait Octavia, Mads suivrait simplement", nous a dit Kai.

J'ai jeté un coup d'œil à Rika alors qu'elle et Banks tenaient les mains de Winter.

"Trouvez-les simplement", a plaidé Winter, le visage gravé de douleur alors que les larmes remplissaient ses yeux. "S'il vous plaît, trouvez-les."

Elle a toujours essayé de le cacher, mais je ne pouvais qu'imaginer à quel point elle se sentait impuissante.

Je me retournai et tombai à genoux devant elle. — Arrête, ai-je dit en lui touchant la main. "Octavia a besoin de te voir sans peur."

Le bateau a rebondi sur l'eau, mes propres yeux larmoyants à cause du vent.

« Si c'était Athos, me dit-elle, tu serais terrifié. Je regardai à nouveau Rika, un regard passant entre nous.

"Quand ce sera Athos, vous serez terrifié", a déclaré Winter.

Comme si ce n'était qu'une question de temps.

Je serrai la mâchoire, n'ayant besoin d'aucune explication sur ce qu'elle voulait dire.

Elle avait raison. Nous avions envoyé les enfants au dojo parce que nous voulions les préparer, mais nous étions si arrogants que nous n'aurions jamais pensé que quelqu'un aurait assez de couilles pour essayer quoi que ce soit.

"Notre vie crée des ennemis", a-t-elle déclaré à voix basse.

Les yeux de Rika se posèrent sur les miens, et là où je voyais habituellement de la force et du réconfort, je vis de l'incertitude. Nous n'avions jamais cessé d'entrer dans la merde, mais nos enfants en danger à cause d'une menace extérieure ne s'étaient jamais produits auparavant.

Cela se reproduirait.

Que devions-nous faire ? Cacher? Être invisible? Vivre tranquillement ?

Se recroqueviller?

Je ne savais pas comment être quelqu'un d'autre.

« Pitom ! » J'ai entendu Will crier.

Je me levai en me retournant.

126

"À peine", a-t-il ajouté. "C'est difficile à distinguer dans la tempête."

Je m'avançai derrière lui, agrippant son épaule pour me soutenir, et regardai par-dessus le pare-brise, voyant la lointaine lueur violette des lumières. Damon se leva de son siège, se préparant. "Dieu merci." « Attends, qu'est-ce que c'est ? » Les banques ont appelé.

Je secouai la tête, suivant son regard.

Me penchant plus près du bord, j'agrippai le côté du bateau, à peine capable de distinguer quelque chose dans l'eau.

« Il y a quelque chose là-bas ! criai-je à Kai en pointant du doigt. "Là bas!"

Kai a tourné le bateau et nous nous sommes rapprochés, le petit vaisseau apparaissant. Les cheveux noirs et un costume noir sont devenus de plus en plus clairs, et Banks a crié: "Mads!"

"Oh mon Dieu." Les jointures de Winter devinrent blanches alors qu'elle agrippait la main de Rika et se redressait. « Est-ce qu'ils vont bien ? Sont-ils blessés ? Est-ce que tu vois
Octavie ?

"Arrête arrête arrête!" insista Damon.

J'ai fixé mon regard sur le gamin dans le bateau, cherchant quoi que ce soit pour dire s'il était blessé, vivant, toujours en danger...

Mais Kai allait trop vite pour s'arrêter en un rien de temps. Il a fait le tour de l'autre hors-bord encore et encore, ralentissant et finissant par se mettre sur le côté.

Le bateau immobile était assis dans l'eau, se balançant d'un côté à l'autre dans le sillage de notre embarcation, et j'ai regardé par-dessus, voyant Mads tenant une petite forme à ses côtés.
Des traînées de sang bordaient le côté de son visage.

Merde.

Je n'ai vu Ilia Oblensky nulle part. Mon estomac nageait et coulait en même temps. Mes mains tremblaient, désespérées d'aller là-bas, parce que si nous ne les avions pas dans nos bras, elles pourraient encore être perdues.

Avant que Will ne puisse nous attacher, Damon sauta dans l'autre bateau et tomba à genoux, prenant les épaules d'Octavia.

Mais ses bras sont restés autour de Madden.

Banks attrapa son fils, le serrant contre elle, mais il ne lâcha pas Tavi. "Est-ce que ça va?" elle a pleuré. "Es-tu blessé?"

Elle essaya de relever son visage et de le regarder, mais il s'éloigna doucement. "Ce n'est pas mon sang," dit-il calmement.

« Octavie ? L'hiver a appelé.

Kai plongea et attrapa le visage de son fils, le gamin paraissant aussi calme que jamais avec un pincement impatient des lèvres.

Ilia Oblensky s'est effondré contre le tableau de bord, donnant l'impression que la vie s'écoulait de lui.

« Des fous ? Kai leva les yeux vers son enfant. « Ça va ? Qu'est-il arrivé? A qui est ce sang ?

L'enfant de onze ans regarda fixement ses parents, ses lèvres tordues sur le côté comme s'il s'ennuyait. Octavia se blottit contre lui, frissonnant.

À part quelques joues rouges et des nez pincés, ils avaient l'air bien.

Kai poussa du sol et tourna son attention vers Ilia, attrapant le col du gars. « Espèce de fils de pute », grogna-t-il. "Tu as mis la main sur mon enfant."

Mais Ilia souffla en respirant, et Kai hésita, laissant ses yeux tomber sur la forme d'Ilia.

Il le relâcha et déchira sa veste. Du sang recouvrait sa chemise noire, ses cheveux blonds moites et emmêlés.

Nous nous sommes tous calmés.

Kai ouvrit d'un coup sec sa chemise, et je remarquai les petits trous et le sang qui en coulait. La couleur s'écoulait du visage d'Ilia alors qu'il commençait à s'estomper. Il avait des minutes.

"Ses poumons sont perforés", a déclaré Kai en se tournant vers nous. "Qu'est-ce qui s'est passé ?"

Et puis à Madden. "Des fous ? Qu'est-il arrivé?"

Kai savait ce qui s'était passé. Nous savions tous. Et Mads n'allait pas répondre à ce qui était déjà évident.

« Elle a froid », fut tout ce qu'il dit.

"Octavia," dit Damon, essayant à nouveau de l'éloigner.

Finalement, elle leva les yeux vers lui. "Papa."

Elle tendit la main vers lui et il la prit dans ses bras, la serrant fort. « Ça va ? » Il a demandé. "Est-ce qu'ils t'ont fait du mal ?"

Elle secoua la tête, ses nattes et tous les bijoux qu'elle avait dans les cheveux scintillant au clair de lune.

Elle tendit la main par-dessus son épaule, dans la nuit. « Pithom », dit-elle en désignant le yacht qui s'estompait de plus en plus à l'horizon.

Les vagues se sont soulevées, nous éclaboussant d'embruns, et j'ai cligné des yeux contre la neige, voyant que la mer commençait à devenir agitée.

« Nous l'obtiendrons », lui assura-t-il.

« Ça s'éloigne », gémit-elle.

Il est remonté sur notre bateau avec elle et l'a mise sur les genoux de sa mère. "Ne vous inquiétez pas."

Emmy et Will sont remontés sur notre vaisseau avec Rika, et je me suis assis sur le siège à côté d'Ilia, redémarrant le moteur.

« Appelle une ambulance », ai-je crié à ma femme.

Elle acquiesça.

Je ne sais pas à quel point cela ferait du bien. Je devrais juste jeter cet enfoiré par-dessus bord maintenant.

Mais je ne refuserais pas ce plaisir à Kai ou Damon. Si les médecins le sauvaient, nous le renverrions au douzième dès qu'il serait prêt.

*Poumons perforés.*Un œil arraché de son orbite. Un cadavre à St. Killian's. J'ai regardé Mads, Kai désespéré de voir son fils effrayé ou avoir besoin de lui, mais...

Kai tenait juste le visage de son fils, essuyant le sang et essayant d'établir un contact visuel.

"Nous allons bien," fut tout ce qu'il dit, cependant.

Kai le fixa, sans aucun doute reconnaissant que les enfants soient en sécurité, mais toujours mal à l'aise.

« Ramenons-les simplement en ville », a dit Banks à son mari. "Ils gèlent."

« Je vais suivre », leur ai-je dit.

Kai a conduit Mads sur l'autre bateau avec Banks, et je les ai laissés sortir d'ici avant de les suivre immédiatement.

La tête d'Ilia pendait, oscillant avec le rebond du bateau, et malgré l'air froid qui se précipitait vers moi, la sueur mouillait ma peau.

Nous les avions trouvés.

Et les mots de Winter revinrent, serpentant dans ma tête.

Notre vie crée des ennemis.

Nous avons choisi cela. Les enfants ne l'ont pas fait.

Quelles étaient nos options ? Se séparer en famille ? Arrêter de construire ? Prendre nos chemins séparés ?

Les enfants étaient en danger, mais les enfants n'en voudraient pas non plus. Ils s'adoraient tous.

Nous avons menacé les autres, mais nous n'avons pas demandé cela. Le comportement des autres pourrait finir par être notre problème… mais pas notre responsabilité.

Nous méritions ce que nous avions, et je n'enseignais pas à Athos – ou à mon fils – qu'ils ne méritaient pas exactement ce qu'ils voulaient. La dernière chose que j'apprendrais à mes enfants était de se recroqueviller, de se cacher ou de fuir.

Nous avons amarré les bateaux, l'ambulance attendant déjà de charger Ilia sur une civière.

Mais j'étais à peu près sûr qu'il était déjà mort.

Ou serait assez tôt.

Emmy a parlé à la police, et je n'étais pas sûr de l'histoire qu'elle leur racontait, mais ils savaient que nous n'irions nulle part. Nous serions là s'ils avaient des questions demain.

« Pouvons-nous encore ouvrir des cadeaux ? Octavia pépia, sa voix joyeuse habituelle en retour.

"Ouais," rit Damon, la serrant à nouveau contre lui.

Il la mit dans la voiture, Mads et Winter grimpant après elle, mais Kai resta en arrière, passant sa main dans ses cheveux.

Comme d'habitude, il s'inquiétait de tout, et je savais de quoi il s'inquiétait.

J'étais inquiète aussi, mais je savais que ce qui se passait dans sa tête était bien plus grand que les doutes dans la mienne.

Je me dirigeai vers lui, Will et Damon nous rejoignant.

"Jésus Christ," murmura Kai, ayant besoin de se vider la tête avant de monter dans la voiture.

« Nous ne savons rien », lui ai-je rappelé.

Il s'énervait toujours avant de savoir qu'il avait quelque chose à craindre.

"'Ce gamin est fou'", a-t-il dit.

Je l'ai étudié. "Quoi?"

"C'est ce que Dinescu a dit quand son globe oculaire pendait hors de sa tête." Il regardait droit devant. « 'Ce gamin est fou.' Tu penses que Madden a aussi tué ce type à la maison ?

Will et Damon sont restés silencieux, et je savais ce que tout le monde pensait. Cela nous a effrayés, mais étions-nous contrariés qu'il l'ait fait?

« Je pense que c'est à cause de lui qu'ils ont échoué ce soir », ai-je dit à Kai en gardant ma voix basse. « Ne fais pas ça. Je me fous de ce qui est arrivé à ces merdes. Et vous ne devriez pas non plus.

Kai secoua la tête. "Michael..."

"Notre vie fait des ennemis", ai-je déclaré. "Notre force menace les gens."

Je regardai autour de moi, établissant un contact visuel avec chacun d'eux. Pendant des années, je ne les ai pas empêchés de faire ce qu'ils voulaient, parce que je voulais qu'ils embrassent ce qu'ils étaient, mais je n'allais pas laisser Kai sentir qu'il avait fait quelque chose de mal, alors que l'alternative était que Mads ne fasse rien et ces enfants étant perdus pour nous à jamais.

« Nous ne changeons pas », leur ai-je dit.

Kai s'avança vers moi, presque furieux. "Et dans dix ans, quand un autre ennemi, ou l'enfant d'un ennemi, viendra nous surprendre à nouveau ?" "Ils ne voudront plus jouer avec votre enfant dans dix ans", a plaisanté Will.

135

"Ce n'est pas drôle !" Kai grogna, ne se souciant pas de qui l'entendait. "Mon enfant-"

"Je n'ai rien cherché de tout ça !" J'ai fini pour lui. "Rien de tout cela n'est de sa faute. Il a fait ce que fait n'importe quel animal sur cette planète quand quelqu'un menace sa vie.

Kai se tut et je ne reculai pas. Je savais de quoi il s'inquiétait. J'ai compris. Et si un intimidateur s'en prenait un jour au dernier nerf de Mads ? Et s'il se battait et causait plus de mal que prévu ?

Et si tout ce qu'il avait appris au dojo et avec son grand-père avait fait de lui quelque chose que nous ne pouvions pas contrôler ?

Mais rien de tout cela n'arriverait.

Pas vraiment.

Mads a appris autant quand se battre que comment se battre. La seule chose qui m'a énervé, c'est à quel point il était plus efficace que moi.

« Maintenant, rentrons à la maison et allumons ce putain d'arbre et bordons nos enfants », leur ai-je dit à tous. "Avec un peu de chance, ce qui s'est passé ce soir se propage comme une traînée de poudre, et quiconque a un boeuf réfléchira à deux fois avant de revenir pour nous ou nos enfants."

"Bon sang ouais," marmonna Damon.

Lui et Will sont partis, grimpant dans les voitures, tandis que Kai et moi restions les yeux fixés.

"Nous le surveillons tous," assurai-je à Kai. "Nous l'élevons tous." Kai n'était pas seul.

Sa mâchoire fléchit.

"Il pourrait être à des millions de kilomètres, vivant en enfer en ce moment", ai-je souligné. "Il a ramené lui-même et cette petite fille à la maison ce soir."

Nous avons appris aux soldats à tuer des gens pour économiser un nickel sur un baril de pétrole.

Quoi que Mads fasse ou ne fasse pas ce soir, il n'avait pas le choix.

Finalement, les yeux de Kai se sont baissés et sa poitrine s'est effondrée alors qu'il acquiesçait.

Mads était en sécurité. C'était tout ce qui comptait.

Nous avons marché jusqu'aux voitures, grimpant dedans.

« Quelqu'un a-t-il dit des cadeaux ? » criai-je en bouclant ma ceinture de sécurité.

Octavia haleta puis glapit, oubliant déjà l'incident, son regard fixé sur la promesse de tout sous l'arbre.

Après avoir récupéré Athos et le reste des enfants, Will a ramené le bus plein, nous sommes retournés à St. Killian pour trouver le gagnant de la chasse au trésor qui attendait et était prêt pour son prix.

Les enfants ont été traînés à l'étage pour se baigner et en pyjama, tandis que Rika et moi avons poussé à travers, présentant la confiance à Tucker Adams et sa petite amie, Amanda Leigh. Pendant que David restait au Pope avec Taylor et Kai, Damon et Will ont fait sortir clandestinement le corps de la maison vers le camion en attente, afin que Lev puisse le livrer au coroner.

Nous avions tellement de merde à gérer demain.

Et d'essayer de se taire.

Une salve d'applaudissements, un toast au champagne des invités restants, et la maison a finalement commencé à se vider après environ quarante-cinq minutes.

Les enfants contournèrent l'arbre de quinze pieds, allumant plus de bougies alors que seules quelques-unes restaient allumées dans toute la maison, le vent extérieur hurlant dans les coins et recoins de la vieille église.

Je me suis reculé, regardant les enfants ouvrir des cadeaux - à l'exception de celui qu'ils avaient gardé pour le jour de Noël - jouer avec leurs jouets, montrer leurs nouveaux gadgets et jeter les livres du côté que nous avons essayé de faire figurer sur chaque liste de vacances, juste au cas où ils s'y intéresseraient.

Damon tenait un paquet enveloppé dans du papier brun, le regardant presque nerveusement, comme s'il n'était pas sûr d'être prêt à l'ouvrir, tandis qu'Octavia courait vers le banc de la fenêtre, se laissant tomber à côté de Madden. Elle a colorié avec ses nouveaux marqueurs Crayola que ses parents avaient refusé de lui confier jusqu'à présent, tandis que Mads dessinait avec ses nouveaux crayons et bloc-notes.

Elle secouait ses jambes d'avant en arrière.

Je glissai mes bras autour de Rika, la serrant contre moi. "Les enfants rebondissent, n'est-ce pas?"

Mon Dieu.

Elle a ri. "Je pense qu'Octavia savait ce que le reste d'entre nous ne savait pas."

"Ce qui était?"

"Elle n'a jamais été vraiment en danger."

J'ai regardé les enfants, Mads dessiner probablement un autre oiseau, alors que son cousin essayait d'agir comme lui avec son marqueur violet.

« Ont-ils attrapé le bateau ? Rika m'a demandé.

"Le temps est trop mauvais." J'embrassai sa tête, ma main posée sur son ventre. "Ils devront attendre jusqu'au matin."

Je me demandai s'il y avait quelqu'un dessus, ou si les trois hommes l'avaient fait tout seuls.

Pour tout ce qui m'importait, j'espérais qu'ils ne le trouveraient jamais. Ce bateau était maudit.

« En a-t-il parlé ? demanda Rika.

Qui?

Mais ensuite j'ai réalisé qu'elle regardait toujours Mads.

J'ai soupiré. "Je doute qu'il le fasse."

Kai a peut-être paniqué, mais je n'étais pas sûr que ce soit enregistré auprès de son fils.

Le sens de l'empathie de Mads n'était pas comme les autres.

Du moins ça j'avais vu.

J'ai regardé la scène, du papier doré et rouge éparpillé sur le sol, tandis que des flammes scintillaient sur l'arbre, les rubans rouges suspendus et si beaux contre les chutes de neige qui tombaient toujours à l'extérieur.

Demain, il y aurait de la nourriture et de la luge, et peut-être du football dans la neige, car s'il y avait une chose que nous savions maintenant, c'était que chaque instant passé ensemble était exactement ce à quoi nous appartenions.

Des friandises ont couvert la table à manger alors qu'un feu brûlait dans la cheminée, et Emmy a commencé un disque. Je souris, resserrant mon emprise sur Rika et espérant que nous n'aurions plus jamais à revivre ce que nous avons traversé ce soir.

Et si nous le faisions, s'il vous plaît, que ce soit dans des années. Mon cœur n'avait toujours pas ralenti.

141

Athos a essayé de jeter un coup d'œil au dessin de Mads, mais il s'est juste détourné alors qu'elle lui ébouriffait les cheveux. Je la regardai marcher et grimper sur le rebord de la fenêtre de l'autre côté de la pièce, sirotant son punch pendant qu'elle regardait tout le monde.

Mon cœur s'est emballé et j'ai failli m'étouffer avec les mots.

"Je t'ai vu nous regarder depuis cette fenêtre il y a tant d'années." J'ai pointé du doigt l'endroit où Athos était maintenant assis, me souvenant que la Nuit du Diable avait si longtemps

depuis. "Essayer de ne pas te sentir là, mais avoir besoin de toi pour rester." Elle appuya sa tête contre mon corps.

« Nous étions à peu près là quand je t'ai envoyé les yeux bandés », lui fis-je remarquer.

"M'a poussé, tu veux dire."

J'ai ri. J'étais tellement con.

J'étais toujours un connard, mais elle m'aimait quand même.

Elle me serra les bras, me serrant en retour. "Je voulais tout ressentir, tant que je pouvais le ressentir avec toi", m'a-t-elle dit. "Toutes ces années plus tard, cela n'a pas changé."

Pas même un pouce.

La musique jouait et les enfants riaient, la plupart inconscients de ce qui s'était passé ce soir, bien que Rika ait mis Athos au courant.

Nous avons créé notre vie ici.

Une vie. Une chance.

« Personne ne nous arrête », murmura-t-elle. "Personne ne nous appartient."

Je la serrai fort. "Et nous ne changeons pas."

Épilogue

Fous

Je me frottai les oreilles, la friction remplissant mes tympans et faisant disparaître le bruit de la fête et me semblant plus éloigné qu'il ne l'était. Maintes et maintes fois, j'ai noyé les bavardages, la vaisselle étant débarrassée en bas, les portes s'ouvrant et se fermant....

J'aimais le bruit. Pluie et oiseaux et vent. Je n'aimais pas le bruit des autres. Cela rendait la pièce petite. Trop petit. Je ne pouvais pas penser.

Après les cadeaux et les friandises, je m'étais glissée dans la salle de bains à l'étage, j'avais fermé la porte et je suis restée là quelques minutes, peut-être plus, à me frotter les oreilles en fermant les yeux. Je détestais que je l'ai fait.

J'ai détesté que ça aide.

Je détestais devoir me cacher pour le faire.

Parce que je détestais la façon dont Ivar me regardait il y a des années quand il m'a surpris en train de le faire.

Je pouvais lire la pièce maintenant. Je savais que je ne serais jamais lui, et je savais quelles parties de moi je devais taire.

Assise sur le rebord de la baignoire et tenant ma tête dans mes mains, j'écoutais ma respiration dans mes oreilles, j'entendais mon pouls, et finalement je sentais que tout ralentissait. Mon coeur. Ma respiration.

Mes pensées.

J'inspirai profondément et expirai lentement, sentant la stabilité et le calme revenir.

Finalement, je me levai de mon siège et me tournai pour faire face au miroir, redressant mes cheveux des deux côtés et repoussant la croissance d'un quart de pouce derrière mes oreilles. Je demanderais à mon père de m'emmener faire une coupe demain. Nous y allions habituellement un samedi sur deux, mais je ne voulais pas attendre.

Versant du savon dans ma paume, je me lavai à nouveau les mains, les essuyai, puis passai mes doigts sur mon costume noir propre et redressai ma cravate, l'habitude de sentir mes vêtements me rassurant. Comme une armure.

Je sortis de la salle de bain et éteignis la lumière, me dirigeant vers la chambre des garçons que nous partagions tous lorsque nous étions restés à St. Killian.

Mais les talons ont touché le sol derrière moi et j'ai entendu la voix de ma mère. "J'ai un pyjama."

Je jetai un coup d'œil par-dessus mon épaule, m'arrêtant et regardant sa robe. J'adorais quand ma mère s'habillait. C'était joli.

"Je vais bien," lui ai-je dit.

Elle plissa les yeux. « Tu ne veux pas dormir dans quelque chose de plus confortable ?

"Je suis à l'aise."

Je m'étais douché à notre retour et j'avais mis un costume neuf.

J'ai recommencé à marcher, mais j'ai entendu son pas vers moi. « Fous, je... »

J'ai secoué la tête. « Non, ne viens pas », lui ai-je dit en me tournant vers elle. "Je veux être seul."

"Je veux m'asseoir avec toi ce soir", m'a-t-elle dit.

Mon estomac noué. C'était la dernière chose dont j'avais besoin. Je savais qu'elle essayait juste de faire ce qu'elle pensait que les parents devraient faire, ou elle supposait que j'avais besoin de quelque chose dont je ne savais pas que j'avais besoin - comme une conversation ou un câlin ou quelque chose comme ça - mais les parents ont tout empiré. Je n'ai pas eu besoin d'aide.

"Je vais bien," dis-je à nouveau.

Ses yeux se plissaient d'inquiétude, et je savais que quoi que je fasse ou dise, elle s'inquiéterait de toute façon.

Je serrai les dents et forçai mes pieds à se déplacer vers elle, plongeant pour une étreinte rapide – lui tapotant le dos deux fois – parce que je savais que cela la ferait se sentir mieux. "Je vais bien," répétai-je.

Me retournant, je me dirigeai vers le couloir, expirant quand je tournai le coin et qu'elle ne m'avait pas rappelé ou ne m'avait pas suivi.

Virant vers la droite, vers la chambre des garçons, j'ai vu mon oncle se balancer au coin du couloir devant moi et s'arrêter, croisant mes yeux.

J'ai arrêté aussi.

147

Quelque chose de bizarre traversa ses yeux noirs, comme un mélange d'amusement et d'intérêt, et je me préparai alors qu'il marchait pour moi.

J'aimais mon oncle Damon. Il n'a pas essayé de me parler tout le temps.

Généralement.

Je l'ai regardé, ma colonne vertébrale se raidissant alors qu'il se penchait pour entrer dans mon visage, la puanteur des cigarettes remplissant mes narines.

"Je sais ce que tu as fait," murmura-t-il, gardant les mots entre nous.

Je l'ai regardé.

« Si jamais mon enfant est en danger, n'hésite pas à recommencer », m'a-t-il dit.

"Comprendre?"

Je suis resté silencieux.

Mais je savais de quoi il parlait.

Je n'ai pas compris la plupart des gens. Ils agissaient comme si la plupart des décisions dans la vie étaient un choix. N'étais-je pas censé faire quoi que ce soit quand ces hommes sont venus ce soir ?

C'est pourquoi j'avais gardé ma bouche fermée. Mes parents auraient paniqué s'ils nous avaient perdus, et ils auraient quand

148

même paniqué s'ils avaient su comment j'avais arrêté ça. Ils m'auraient juste confondu. Je ne savais pas ce qu'ils voulaient.

Mais oncle Damon ne voulait pas me faire répondre à une question à laquelle il avait déjà été confronté à la réponse.

Et il ne semblait pas fâché.

« Tu as des sentiments négatifs à propos de ce qui s'est passé ce soir ? » il m'a demandé.

J'ai baissé les yeux.

Le mensonge inquiéterait mes parents. La vérité les inquiéterait davantage.

"Ouais, je ne le pensais pas." Il sourit. « Si jamais tu le fais, tu viens me voir. J'ai compris?"

Cela a pris un moment, mais j'ai hoché la tête.

Il a plongé et a laissé un bisou sur ma joue avant de se relever et de continuer son chemin.

J'ai attendu qu'il soit au coin de la rue avant de sortir le mouchoir de ma poche et d'essuyer les crachats de tabac sur ma peau.

Rembourrant le tissu dans mon pantalon, j'entrai dans la chambre sombre. Ivarsen et moi étions de l'autre côté de la pièce dans des lits simples, et Gunnar était dans le lit à

149

côté du mien, ses couvertures autour des pieds.

Dag et Fane étaient dans leur coin du grenier, tandis que les filles étaient à côté.

Mais alors que je me dirigeais vers mon lit, j'ai repéré une bosse sous les couvertures. Je me rapprochai, voyant de longs cheveux noirs se déployer sur mon oreiller.

Octavie.

Je m'arrêtai, la sentant d'ici. Sa mère lui a acheté son propre shampoing qui semblait s'infiltrer dans tout ce qu'elle possédait - et tout ce que je possédais quand elle était proche.

Je n'étais pas assez vieux pour me souvenir de la naissance de Jett, mais quand Octavia est arrivée, c'était la première fois que je me souvenais de la présence d'un bébé. Parfait et fragile et déjà aimé de tous, peu importe qui il serait quand il grandirait.

J'ai été comme ça une fois aussi. Avant que les gens ne me connaissent.

Je serrai les poings en voyant le bleu sur son bras.

Tous les autres m'ont forcé à venir ici ou à y aller et à faire partie des choses. Octavia quittait toujours ce qu'elle faisait ou avec qui elle était et venait me voir à la place. C'était sympa.

Elle remua, inspira et se retourna sur le dos.

Je retirai l'oreiller de sous elle, sa tête tombant sur le lit alors que je posais l'oreiller sur le côté. "Tu es dans mon lit."

Je m'effondrai à côté d'elle et appuyai ma tête sur l'oreiller contre la tête de lit.

En fouillant dans ma poche de poitrine, j'ai sorti quelques carrés de papier à croquis et j'ai commencé à plier.

Elle se blottit contre moi, posant sa tête sur mon bras.

"Es tu effrayé?" lui demandai-je sans détourner les yeux de mon origami.

"J'étais un peu avant." Sa petite voix, si petite, me fit mal à la poitrine.

Ma main ralentit un instant et je déglutis. Elle a été éloignée de moi, sortie de la maison et sortie dans l'océan dans une tempête de neige ce soir.

Mais ce n'était peut-être pas eux qui lui faisaient peur.

Elle a tout vu.

Tout.

« Pourquoi as-tu eu peur ? » ai-je demandé, mais je n'ai pas respiré en attendant la réponse.

Elle bougea, me regardant. « N'est-ce pas ? »

Je n'ai rien dit, j'ai simplement continué à plier la colombe alors que sa chaleur filtrait à travers le bras de ma veste.

Un peu.

Je me suis raclé la gorge. « N'ayez pas peur. Cela n'arrivera plus jamais.

"Comment savez-vous?"

J'ai terminé l'oiseau, le tenant contre l'ombre des chutes de neige au plafond.

"Parce que la prochaine fois, je serai plus grand," dis-je.

Me tournant vers elle, je plaçai l'oiseau sous son menton, voyant son sourire apparaître, et tirai les couvertures, la bordant.

« Ils trouveront Pithom », lui ai-je dit. "Ne vous inquiétez pas."

Elle se recroquevilla, fermant les yeux. "Ils ne le trouveront pas."

"Pourquoi pas?"

"C'est ce que je souhaitais sur la feuille de basilic", a-t-elle expliqué. "Un vaisseau fantôme." Un vaisseau fantôme. Je gardai

152

la bouche fermée, ne voulant pas faire éclater sa bulle.

Pithom était un yacht avec un système de suivi. Il ne resterait pas perdu longtemps.

« Je vais le trouver un jour », a-t-elle déclaré.

Ouais ok.

Je la regardai, ses cils noirs drapés sur sa peau pâle, et je souhaitais presque que cela puisse arriver pour elle. Son imagination était pleine de choses merveilleuses, et je n'avais aucune imagination du tout. Je ne voulais pas qu'elle soit comme moi.

Les aventures dans sa tête ressemblaient à un monde différent.

Je levai la main pour écarter la mèche de cheveux sur sa joue, mais je m'arrêtai, relâchant mon bras.

J'ai forcé la boule dans ma gorge alors que je la regardais. "Puis-je venir?" J'ai chuchoté.

« Il n'y a rien que tu aimes en mer, terrien », taquina-t-elle, les yeux toujours fermés. "Pas d'oiseaux."

Je me suis détourné. Il y a quelques oiseaux.

Je n'avais jamais vraiment envie d'aller nulle part ou de voir le monde. J'aimais être à la maison, partout où je n'avais pas à faire face à des gens ou à rencontrer de nouvelles personnes. Mais si elle partait… « Puis-je venir ? J'ai demandé à nouveau.

Elle hocha la tête en bâillant. "Mm-hmm. Mais je suis capitaine. Je réprimai mon sourire en la regardant s'endormir.

Navire ou pas navire, elle était le capitaine de tout le monde, et elle le savait.

Debout, je resserrai les couvertures sur elle, les glissant sous le matelas pour les maintenir en place.

Me levant, je regardai Octavia, la colombe en origami toujours sous son menton. L'ecchymose violette sur son bras, due à l'une des mains des hommes, ressortait, sombre et visible, même dans le faible clair de lune traversant la fenêtre.

Je fléchis la mâchoire, resserrant ma cravate et lissant à nouveau mes cheveux.

*Avez-vous des sentiments négatifs à propos de ce soir ?*avait-il demandé.

J'avais tout le temps de mauvais sentiments. Quand la musique était trop forte. Quand les chiens de ma mère ont eu des poils sur mon lit. Lorsque Marina préparait un plat différemment, je comptais sur elle pour toujours le préparer comme je l'aimais.

J'ai regardé Octavia dormir.

J'avais de mauvais sentiments quand on m'enlevait des choses.

Pas à propos d'autres choses.

Je levai la main, inspectant la saleté sous mon ongle.

En utilisant mon pouce, je l'ai choisi, remarquant qu'il était rouge.

J'expirai, mon cœur battant dans ma poitrine.

Sortant mon mouchoir, j'essuyai ma main et me dirigeai vers la fenêtre, fouillant dans ma poche de poitrine et retirant la feuille de basilic de tout à l'heure.

Je ne l'avais pas brûlé.

La glissant entre mes lèvres et dans ma bouche, j'ai mâché la feuille et l'ai avalée, le chatouillement dans ma gorge atteignant mon estomac alors que le goût piquant recouvrait ma langue.

Je me tournai pour m'asseoir dans le fauteuil, me contentant d'y dormir pour la nuit et de garder un œil ouvert, mais quelque chose brillait au-dessus de moi et je levai les yeux.

Une clé était accrochée à la serrure de la fenêtre, un petit rouleau de papier niché dans la chaîne.

J'ai regardé autour de moi dans la pièce, me demandant à qui elle appartenait.

Levant la main, je décrochai la chaîne de la serrure, tenant le passe-partout dans ma main et retirant le papier du maillon.

En le déroulant, je lis une écriture noire. "Les accords du cœur doivent être touchés pour être joués."

Je plissa les yeux en le lisant à nouveau. Je n'étais pas sûr de ce qu'il me disait. Peut-être que ça ne m'était même pas destiné.

J'ai inspecté la vieille clé rouillée et le porte-clés, ce qui ressemblait à un encensoir suspendu au bout.

J'ai fait une pause. Les Thuribles servaient à répandre de l'encens à la messe. La cathédrale du village en possédait une immense.

Mon visage est tombé. C'était un indice. Les pensées et les théories envahissaient mon cerveau.

Je regardai Octavia par-dessus mon épaule, sachant à quel point elle aimerait une aventure. Une chasse. Cette clé est allée à quelque chose. Peut-être un trésor ?

"Les accords du cœur doivent être touchés pour être joués", ai-je récité à nouveau, essayant de comprendre ce que cela signifiait.

Puis ça m'a frappé. Personne n'est à l'abri de l'émotion lorsque ces accords sont tirés.

Personne.

Je fermai les yeux, sentant le sang sous mes ongles alors que j'enroulais mes doigts froids autour de la clé.

Une nuit bientôt.

Pendant que tout le monde dormait.

On va découvrir ce que la clé ouvre, Octavia. La nuit nous appartiendra.

LA FIN

www.ingramcontent.com/pod-product-compliance
Lightning Source LLC
Chambersburg PA
CBHW071326140726
47996CB00005B/1837